S0-DRG-084

Manage Your Career

Manage Your Career

10 Keys to Survival and Success When Interviewing and on the Job

Second Edition

Vijay Sathe

 BUSINESS EXPERT PRESS

Manage Your Career: 10 Keys to Survival and Success When Interviewing and on the Job, Second Edition
Copyright © Business Expert Press, LLC, 2015.

All rights reserved. No part of this publication may be reproduced, stored in a retrieval system, or transmitted in any form or by any means—electronic, mechanical, photocopy, recording, or any other except for brief quotations, not to exceed 400 words, without the prior permission of the publisher.

First published in 2015 by
Business Expert Press, LLC
222 East 46th Street, New York, NY 10017
www.businessexpertpress.com

ISBN-13: 978-1-63157-061-2 (paperback)
ISBN-13: 978-1-63157-062-9 (e-book)

Business Expert Press Human Resource Management and Organizational Behavior Collection

Collection ISSN: 1946-5637 (print)
Collection ISSN: 1946-5645 (electronic)

Cover and interior design by S4Carlisle Publishing Services Private Ltd., Chennai, India

First edition: August 2008

10 9 8 7 6 5 4 3 2 1

Printed in the United States of America.

Dedication

For Judah and Rowan

Abstract

This book gives you the keys to survival and success as your career progresses from one job to the next in the same organization or in different organizations—be they for-profit, nonprofit, government, or volunteer. It can help you to avoid the many traps and pitfalls you will encounter along your career path and guide you toward increased personal effectiveness during all three stages of the job cycle—when you are interviewing for a new job, as a newcomer, and thereafter.

Whether you are preparing to enter the workforce for the first time or are in an early, middle, or a later career stage, this book will show you how to avoid jobs and organizations that are not right for you. It will also help you to go beyond survival to achieve *success* by doing your job well and making other contributions to your organization in ways that improve your job performance, job satisfaction, happiness at work, and personal and professional growth.

The keys this book provides work whether you are an independent contributor, a manager responsible for the work of others, or an executive responsible for the enterprise. Organizational leaders, human resource professionals, career coaches, and mentors can also use this book to educate and train people to make work more productive and personally rewarding for themselves and others for whom they are responsible.

Keywords

career management, credibility, culture, culture fit, entrepreneurship, interviewing, job search, leadership, management, relationships

Contents

Figures, Exhibits, and Arts

Preface

This book is based on a course that I have developed and taught MBAs and executives over the last 30 years, on how to manage their careers by creating a positive impact for their organizations and for themselves. The theory of the book is derived from the scholarly literature and the detailed case studies developed for the course.*

Students from around the world have used the fundamentals of this book. How one behaves and what one believes may differ greatly across national cultures, of course, but the *concepts, frameworks,* and *tools* presented in this book have been validated by hundreds of people from all corners of the globe.[1] The stories included in the book are not fiction but real-life examples drawn from the personal experience of these people, from the cases developed for the course, and from my research and consulting work.

The Introduction to this second edition includes a new section on "A Theory of Success" that more clearly shows how the 10 keys to survival and success, which are at the heart of this book, together influence your job performance, job satisfaction, happiness at work, and personal and professional growth.

New in this second edition is Part V, on how these 10 keys work for those who do not work in an organization. Increasing numbers of people in the workforce are neither employees nor employers. They are what I call "solo operators." Donna Finley, an exemplary solo operator, reflects on her experience and shows how she has applied the 10 keys to achieve success.

Also new, at the end of the book, is my "secret sauce for career success" derived from 30 years of teaching the course on which this book is based. Tongue-in-cheek, of course, I give this "recipe" to participants at the end

---

*A brief description of some of these cases, available through Harvard Business School Publishing, is included in Appendix 2 at the end of the book, as are the notes for scholars and others interested in the literature.

of the course, and the positive feedback I have received leads me to offer it to you in this second edition.

A template for self-reflection and a model self-reflection paper written by James Pike that illustrates how to use it are included in Appendix 1. If you write a self-reflection paper using this template and, if possible, receive feedback on it from your course instructor or career coach, you may gain new insights that help you to improve your job performance, job satisfaction, happiness at work, and personal and professional growth.

I wish to thank Irwin/McGraw-Hill for the adaptation and use of some of the material originally published in my book *Culture and Related Corporate Realities*, which is now out of print. Kristina Patten provided valuable faculty support.

There is not enough space here to list all of the other people I want to thank, but I would like to acknowledge the inspiration, the intellectual challenge, and the support received from Mike Csikszentmihalyi and Dick Ellsworth. They influenced this work by their scholarship and colleagueship more than they know.

I thank Jeffery Schidlowsky for the art he has produced for this second edition. The six images he has created appear at different points in the book to visually reinforce six key messages of the book. My thanks also to Donna Finley for her reflections as a solo operator, and to James Pike for his self-reflection paper.

I want to express my appreciation to the hundreds of students who have taken this course and from whom I have learned so much. They provided valuable feedback and encouraged me to publish this book. All errors that remain are of course mine. The learning goes on.

Claremont, California
May 2015

Advance Quotes From The First Edition

Professor Sathe is a great gift, a passionate teacher who cares deeply about the life arc of each individual student. In his vibrant classroom, he translates strategic management into a personal discipline—and here in these pages, he brings to you and me the benefits of his wise mentorship.

—Jim Collins, author of *Good to Great*

Vijay Sathe is one of the great teachers of our time. His work will help many readers improve their personal situation. A must-read for those who want to increase their personal effectiveness.

—Stephen Drotter, President, Drotter Human Resources and co-author of *The Leadership Pipeline*

Vijay Sathe offers in this book his unique advice for achieving success throughout our careers. But he does more than that. By sharing his values and helping clarify ours, he inspires us to go beyond success and build a wonderful life of meaning and purpose.

—Claudio Fernández-Aráoz, Partner of Egon Zehnder International and author of *Great People Decisions*

I sat in on Vijay Sathe's course at the Drucker School of Management and learned firsthand why it got such rave reviews. With this book, the life-changing messages of the course can now radiate everywhere.

—Justin Menkes, Spencer Stuart, author of *Executive Intelligence*

Written by a world-renowned expert on culture, *Manage Your Career* shows the job seeker how to choose an employer that is a culture fit. Almost nothing could be more important in determining job satisfaction and performance.

—Geoff Smart, Chairman and CEO of ghSMART and author of *Who*

Imagine inviting an acclaimed business school professor and one of the world's top management experts into your office to help guide you through your entire career, steering you from start to finish. Vijay Sathe is not only a hugely respected management consultant; he's one of a rare few who have also tested and refined his ideas in rigorous academic environments over the last 30 years. By reading this book, be assured that you have hired the very best to help you navigate through the many challenges and opportunities that you will face throughout your working experience.

—Rabbi Robert Wegbreit, PhD, Educational Director of Yeshivas Bircas HaTorah, Israel

Introduction

If you type "manage your career" or "career management" and search any online bookstore, a long list of books will appear. Most of them deal with career planning, career development, and career choice.[1]

This book is not about career options or the career that is right for you, but it gives you the keys to survival and success in any job, in any organization, as your career progresses from one job to the next in the same organization or in different organizations—be they for-profit, nonprofit, government, or volunteer.[2]

Knowing the keys to survival and success will help you to avoid jobs and organizations that are not right for you. You can also determine if the job and organization you are currently in is right for you, and what you must do to survive and succeed in it.

Even if you do not work in an organization, you probably deal with people who do—they could be your customers, suppliers, or partners. A better understanding of the challenges these people face in their jobs will help you to deal with them more effectively.

The meaning of *survival* in an organization is clear. But survival is merely the entry ticket for *success*, which this book defines as doing your job well and making other contributions to your organization in ways that also create a positive impact for yourself.

There are two types of contributions you can make[3]: (1) results that meet or exceed the performance goals for which you are held accountable and (2) good organizational citizenship, which means contributions beyond your job responsibilities that help the organization.[4]

Both types of contributions are *not* the activities you perform but the *results* you deliver for the organization. It is easy to fall into the activity trap.[5] If you are a sales person, for example, your contribution is not the number of sales calls you make per week but how many dollars of sales you generate. When it is difficult to quantify results, the danger of falling into the activity trap is even greater. For your contribution in developing other people, for example, it is easy to count the number of days of training you provided for them, but did they develop new knowledge or skills as a result? Even a rough qualitative assessment of the latter is more meaningful than a precise quantitative measurement of the former.

As you perform your job and make other contributions to the organization, are you also creating a positive impact for yourself?[6] Outcomes to consider are your job security, job satisfaction, happiness at work,[7] personal and professional growth, and anything else that is important to you.

The terms "job satisfaction" and "happiness at work" are often used interchangeably, but there is a subtle yet important distinction. Satisfaction refers to your cognitive state; it taps how you *think* about your job. Happiness refers to your emotional state; it taps how you *feel* about your work.[8] People don't generally use the term "happiness" in the context of work because it has been viewed as something one has to do to earn a living rather than as something to look forward to or enjoy. But in our knowledge economy, workplaces are not the repetitive work factories of the industrial age. Today's workers recognize that work can and should be fun. Some workers, especially knowledge workers, even demand it!

Where would you place yourself in Figure 1 for your current job and organization? Consider the possible outcomes. If you create a positive impact for yourself but hurt the organization in the process you are being a *sadist*. If your job performance and other contributions to the organization are accomplished through actions that hurt you, the image this conjures up is of the *kamikaze* fighter pilots of World War II. *Stagnation* occurs if you have zero impact on the organization and on yourself. The *disaster zone* is worse—your actions hurt not only yourself but the organization as well. You achieve *success* when you perform your job well and make other contributions to the organization while creating a positive impact for yourself.

Keys and Key Players

To be successful, you must manage your career by thinking about your own needs and also the needs of the organization, and contribute in ways that satisfy both. The 10 keys described in this book can help you to make such contributions.

To use these keys, you must identify the people both inside and outside the organization who are important to your survival and success.

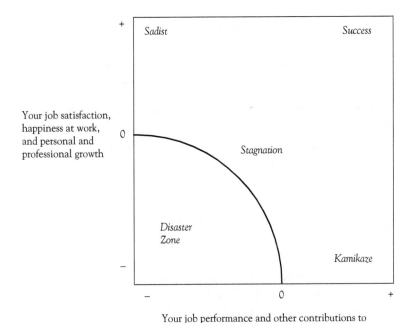

Figure 1 Where would you place yourself in this figure for your current job and organization?

As shown in Exhibit 1, these people typically include (1) your boss, sub-ordinates, peers, clients, and others whom *you serve or depend on* to do your job; (2) mentors, sponsors, champions, and others who have a stake in your success; and (3) your boss's boss and others with whom you do not work directly, but whose opinions and impressions of you count.

From all of these people, *the few who matter the most* for your survival and success are your *key players*. Make a short list of your key players and give them the attention they deserve. The list will change, so review Exhibit 1 periodically and think about your key players and others who are important to your survival and success.

Outline of the Book: The 10 Keys to Survival and Success

Part I gives you the keys to creating a positive impact for your organization and yourself in any job, in any organization. Key #1 provides the concepts, frameworks, and tools for assessing your fit with the key players

Exhibit 1

Your key players and others who are important to your survival and success

I. Think about the people who are important to your survival and success

- (a) Your boss, subordinates, peers, clients, and others whom you *serve or depend on* to do your job
- (b) Mentors, sponsors, champions, and others who have a stake in your success
- (c) Your boss's boss and others whose opinions and impressions of you count
- (d) Any others?

II. From those above, who are the few people who matter the most to your survival and success?

- These are your key players
- Keep the list short (6 or fewer people if possible) and give them the attention they deserve

  1. _____ 2. _____ 3. _____
  4. _____ 5. _____ 6. _____

III. Review I and II periodically and update your list of key players

and with the organization's culture because this influences you and your ability to contribute to the organization.

Key #2 helps you to assess whether your skills, the effort you put in, and the support you receive to do your job are adequate given the challenges of your job. A mismatch hurts you and your ability to contribute to the organization.

Key #3 is the quality of your relationships with the key players and others who are important to your survival and success (Exhibit 1). This is the master key because it opens the doors to both the support you receive to do your job (Key #2) and your credibility (Key #4).

Key #4 is your credibility in the eyes of the key players and others who are important to your survival and success. It is based on your job performance and other contributions and also on how these people *perceive* your contributions, which in turn is influenced by the quality of your relationships with them. Just as a good credit rating offers a financial cushion in managing your personal affairs, your credibility gives you an organizational cushion to try new things and take necessary risks in order to create a positive impact for your organization and yourself.

The rest of the book is organized according to the life cycle of a job. As you move from one job to the next in your career, it helps to understand the organization and the job you are considering moving to *before* you accept the offer (Part II). After starting in the new job, the challenge is to survive and contribute as a newcomer (Part III), and then broaden and deepen your positive impact on your organization and yourself over time (Part IV). The keys to doing all of this are as follows.

In Part II, Key #5 provides insight into what you need to know about your organization, your job, and yourself *before* you accept a new job. Key #6 deals with several recruiting traps and how to avoid them while interviewing for a new job.

In Part III, Key #7 covers the special challenges you must address as a newcomer, and Key #8 offers guidance for monitoring your progress in a new organization and then settling in or moving on.

Part IV covers several important ways in which you can continue to deliver results and make other contributions to create a positive impact on your organization and yourself as your career progresses. Key #9 is for delivering high performance and making other valued contributions to your organization even if you are a misfit in its culture, for taking necessary action that violates its cultural norms, and for managing conflict in order to do what is right.

Key #10 turns to other important ways for creating a positive impact for your organization and yourself—by becoming a manager, a leader, and an entrepreneur. According to conventional wisdom, one person cannot become all three. But just as the "triple-threat" quarterback in American football can kick the ball, throw a pass, and run with the ball, you can contribute as a manager, as a leader, and as an entrepreneur—in ways that help both the organization and yourself.

A Theory of Success: How the 10 Keys Together Influence Your Success

The higher your credibility in the organization (Key #4) when accepting a new job, and ...

The better the diagnosis that you have conducted *prior to* accepting this new job (Key #5) and the more you have avoided the traps that derail the recruiting process (Key #6), and …

The lower your misfit (gap) with your key players and with the organization's culture (Key #1), and the lower your misfit (gap) with the skills, effort, and support that you will require to successfully address your job challenges (Key #2), and …

The better your onboarding into the organization (Keys #7 and #8), and …

The better your development of relationships with your key players and others (Key #3, which is the master key) in order to bridge the values gap with them and with the organization's culture, and …

The greater the improvement in your skills, effort, and support to close the gap with what is required to be successful given your job challenges, and …

The better your results and the greater your other contributions to your organization as an individual contributor (Key #9) and as a manager, leader, and entrepreneur (Key #10), …

The more your credibility (Key #4) will grow in the organization—feedback loop to your credibility (Key #4) when accepting a new job.

Part V is for "solo operators" who are neither employees nor employers. If you are one of them, or become one in the future, the 10 keys are still important for you, but how they are to be applied will vary depending on your particular situation. An exemplary solo operator shows how she has done this to achieve success.

Part VI contains my "secret sauce" for career success. The summary "recipe" provided here looks easy to do but it is in fact very hard to do on a day-to-day basis. There are no guarantees in life or at work, of course, but the closer you get to this ideal, the better your prospects for successful job performance, job satisfaction, happiness at work, and personal and professional growth.

The Importance of Relationships and Their Difficulties

The master key to survival and success in any job, in any organization, is the quality of your relationships (Key #3) with the key players and others (Exhibit 1). The fundamental reason for this is the fact that an organization is a society of human beings who must work together to achieve a common goal, and relationships are at the core of what it means to be human. Some would say they are the very essence of being human.[9]

But this is a huge hang-up for some people who like to work by themselves, take pride in what they produce on their own, and view good relationships as "politics" or as something to be avoided. I know many engineers and computer programmers, for example, who feel this way. I have also met entrepreneurially minded people in established companies who think relationships and politics are holding them back. Would these people be better off if they did not work in an organization?

The reality is that even those who work on their own need to have good relationships with others they deal with—for example, their customers, suppliers, and partners. Perhaps only some artists, scientists, and others who truly work solo can afford to ignore their relationships with others and let their work speak for them instead. All others must come to terms with the importance of good relationships if they want to survive and succeed in their jobs, whether they work in an organization or not.[10] One of the difficulties with this is that some workplaces tolerate bullies, creeps, and backstabbers—the popular term is "jerks"—who inflict harm on others. There is a real danger of labeling someone a "jerk" just because you don't like that person, but what if you are not falling into this trap of stereotyping and feel that one or more of your key players or others are behaving like jerks? I think it is naïve to talk about building good relationships with people who are behaving in this way. If it is not an isolated problem but a pervasive one beyond repair, it may be best to find a better place to work if you can.

There is also the danger of compromising your ideals in the service of good relationships. To avoid this fate, you must determine if you have an *irreconcilable* misfit with the values of the key players or with the organization's culture. If you do, it is best to move on if you can. If you stay in such an organization, you may become what you initially despised.[11] The way forward is to avoid irreconcilable misfits and to deal with others constructively by building good relationships to the furthest extent possible.

PART I

Strive to Create a Positive Impact for Your Organization and Yourself

The first three keys to creating a positive impact for your organization and yourself in any job, in any organization are (1) your fit with the key players and with the organization's culture; (2) your job challenges in relation to your skills, your effort, and the support you receive to do your job; and (3) the quality of your relationships with the key players and others who are important to your survival and success (Figure 2).

Key #1 examines your *fit* with the key players and with the organization's culture—that is, the extent to which your beliefs and values are compatible with those of your key players and of others in the organization. The worse your fit, the more difficult it is for you to create a positive

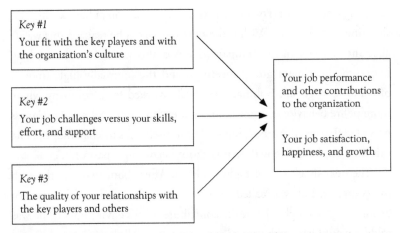

Figure 2 The keys to creating a positive impact for your organization and yourself

impact for your organization and yourself. You will not survive and succeed if your misfit (your "values gap" with the key players and with the organization's culture) is *irreconcilable*. If at all possible, you must avoid such an unbridgeable "values gap."

Key #2 asks whether your skills, the effort you put in, and the support you receive to do your job are adequate given its challenges. If yes, you can perform the job well and enjoy doing it. If not—if there is a "skills, effort, and support gap"—your performance, satisfaction, happiness, and growth will suffer.

Key #3 considers the quality of your relationships with the key players and others who are important to your survival and success. The better your relationships with these people, the more they will support you, and the greater will be your credibility with them. Key #3 is the master key, because it can help you to bridge both your "values gap" and your "skills, effort, and support gap."

Your credibility (Key #4) is your credit rating in the eyes of the key players and others. It is based on your job performance and other contributions and on how these people *perceive* these contributions. It can help you to undertake important initiatives that are innovative or politically risky, because the key players and others will support you and even run interference if you have sufficient credibility with them.

The experience of Bob Drake, a new manager, will be used for illustration throughout the book. Here, briefly, is his story.

The first unpleasant surprise for Bob came on his third day with the company when he heard two senior colleagues arguing in public, cursing and shouting at each other. Within the next few weeks he realized this wasn't aberrant behavior in the company. He was also struck by the very long hours, the infrequent group meetings, and the unusually high amount of rumor and gossip. Bob had previously worked for a company where more polite behavior, shorter hours, more team play, and more openness prevailed. He was disturbed, but said to himself, "It's too bad they operate this way, but I can live with that without becoming a part of it."

The next shock was of higher voltage. After about two months with the company, Bob was called into his boss's office and told he was not being "tough enough." To "really contribute in this environment," he was told he would have to become "more aggressive." Bob was upset but said nothing. For one who prided himself on his competence, the last thing he felt he needed was advice on personal style.

Bob decided he would redouble his efforts to show these people what he could contribute. A large part of Bob's job involved dealings with peers in another department, and he decided to show them what he could contribute by putting in long hours with them and going out of his way to help them. What Bob experienced, however, was fierce internal competition and the withholding of important information; appeals to various parties were to no avail. At his 6 months' performance review Bob's boss told him that he had failed to learn from the feedback given earlier. This was open competition, he was told, and he was not measuring up. Bob got an unsatisfactory rating and was fired.

KEY #1

Your Fit With the Key Players and With the Organization's Culture

The first key is the extent to which your beliefs and values are compatible with those of the key players and with the organization's culture.[1] The better your fit with the key players and with the organization's culture, the easier it will be for you to create positive outcomes for your organization and yourself (Figure 3). However, a "perfect fit" is not generally possible because the key players and the organization's culture can differ from you in many obvious and subtle ways. The bigger your "values gap" with the key players and with the organization's culture, the more difficult it will be for you to create a positive impact for your organization and

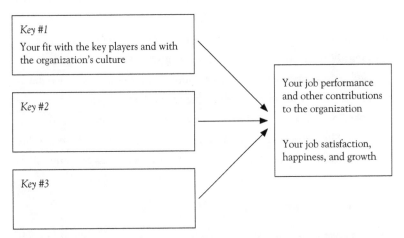

Figure 3 Your ability to create a positive impact for your organization and yourself depends on your fit with the key players and with the organization's culture

for yourself. You must assess the extent of your misfit ("values gap") and determine if it is *irreconcilable* ("unbridgeable").

For example, Bob Drake, the new manager, valued teamwork and a cooperative environment. The key players in his organization believed in cutthroat internal competition. Bob's misfit with them was irreconcilable; he was unable to survive, let alone to succeed in the organization.

Your list of the key players may change over time (see Exhibit 1, page 4), and your fit with them and with the organization's culture could get worse or better if their beliefs and values, or yours, change. It is important to assess your fit not only before and after joining an organization but also on a periodic basis thereafter.

If you have an *irreconcilable* misfit with the key players or with the organization's culture, it is generally best to move on if you can. Other types of misfits must be managed constructively, as described later.

To assess your fit with the key players and with the organization's culture, you need to determine the extent to which your personal beliefs and values are compatible with theirs. Key #1 provides the concepts, frameworks, and tools for making these assessments.

Beliefs and Values

Beliefs are assumptions about the world and how it works. They derive from personal experience and are reinforced by it. Individuals also rely to some degree on the judgment and expertise of others whom they trust, or can identify with, to help them decide what to believe or not to believe.

Values are a special class of beliefs, called *evaluative* beliefs. These are assumptions about what ideals are desirable or worth striving for. Values derive from personal experience and identification with those who have had an important influence on a person's development since early childhood. Values represent preferences for ultimate end states, such as fairness or compassion.[2]

Personal Beliefs and Values

Your *espoused* beliefs and values are what you *say* (to yourself and to others) are your beliefs and values. However, you may not even be aware of your unconscious beliefs and values. Timothy Wilson explains in *Strangers to Ourselves*, his authoritative and highly readable book on what we know about the unconscious mind (2002, pp. 6–8), as follows[3]:

> According to the modern perspective, Freud's view of the unconscious was far too limited. . . . The mind operates most efficiently by relegating a good deal of high-level sophisticated thinking to the unconscious, just as a modern jumbo jetliner is able to fly on automatic pilot with little or no input from the human, "conscious" pilot. . . . It is best to think of the adaptive unconscious as a collection of city-states of the human mind and not as a single, homunculus like the Wizard of Oz, pulling strings behind the curtain of conscious awareness.
>
> Freud argued that our primitive urges do not reach consciousness because they are unacceptable to our more rational, conscious selves and to society at large. . . . According to the modern view, there is a simpler reason for the existence of unconscious mental processes . . . these parts of the mind are inaccessible to conscious awareness— quite possibly because they evolved before consciousness did.

Your unconscious beliefs and values may be revealed (to you and others) by observing your behavior and in particular the *choices* you make over time.[4]

Value System

The relative *ordering* of values is what distinguishes one person's value system from another's. Two people may hold many of the same values, but when these values come into conflict, the individuals may prioritize them very differently.[5]

For example, Bob Drake and the key players in his organization believed that internal competition and cooperation were important for the effective functioning of an organization. However, the others considered internal competition far more important—it ranked far above cooperation in their value system. But for Drake, cooperation was much more important. Drake and the key players had very different value systems.

We sometimes don't realize what it is we really value till we don't have it. For example, money was less important to Drake than he thought prior to joining the organization; a congenial work environment was more important to him than he had realized. Thus, our value system gets tested and clarified—and our values sometimes get reordered—when we reflect on the choices we make as we live our lives.

The following classification scheme developed by the German philosopher Eduard Spranger, comprising six ideal types of person, is an illustration of how different people rank their values differently[6]:

1. The *theoretical* person is primarily interested in the discovery of truth and the systematic ordering of knowledge. The person's interests are empirical, critical, and rational. Scientists or philosophers are often of this type (but not exclusively so).
2. The *economic* person is primarily oriented toward what is useful. He or she is interested in the practical affairs of the business world: in the production, marketing, and consumption of goods; in the use of economic resources; and in the accumulation of tangible wealth.
3. The *aesthetic* person finds chief interest in the artistic aspects of life, without necessarily being a creative artist. This person values form and harmony, and views experience in terms of grace and symmetry.
4. The essential value for the *social* person is love of people—the altruistic or philanthropic aspect of love. People are valued as ends, and the person tends to be kind, sympathetic, and unselfish.
5. The *political* person is characteristically oriented toward power, not necessarily in politics but in whatever area he or she functions.
6. The *religious* person seeks to relate to the universe in a meaningful way and has a spiritual orientation.

Which of these six types of person best describes you? A *social* person or an *economic* person best described Bob Drake; he would have been a much better fit with the key players in his organization if he had been a *political* person.

Do Personal Beliefs and Values Change?

Beliefs do change, but not easily. Values (evaluative beliefs) are even harder to change because they cannot be proven wrong with evidence. For example, the belief that "the earth is flat" can be proven wrong by presenting disconfirming evidence—although history shows this was no easy task, even after the data were available! In contrast, the value that "one must be compassionate" cannot be proven wrong by presenting evidence.

Important personal values rarely change. It typically takes a life-transforming event—such as financial bankruptcy, loss of a loved one, or a similar traumatic personal experience—to produce value change.

Organization's Culture

An organization's *culture* is the set of important beliefs and values that members of the organization share in common. Important beliefs and values are those that are widely enough shared and highly enough placed relative to other shared beliefs and values so as to have a major impact on how members of the organization think, feel, behave, and justify their actions.[7]

To understand how beliefs and values come to be widely shared and clearly ordered, we need to go back to the organization's founding. Since it survived and grew to its present state, the organization *must* have developed a "theory of the business" that worked[8]—otherwise the organization would have ceased to exist. Such a theory consists of the beliefs about how members of the organization must work together to serve customers and other external constituents in return for their support, and the values that are more or less important in doing so. As the organization evolves, these beliefs and values become widely shared and clearly ordered based on what seems to work and what does not.[9]

Culture Types

Every organization has a distinct culture (i.e., a specific set of shared beliefs and values) based on the founding values and subsequent experience, but cultures can also be grouped into types. One such classification scheme (Figure 4) is from the work of Roger Harrison, who described four culture types as follows[10]:

1. *Power orientation*—the desire to dominate the environment and vanquish all opposition, organizational life being principally governed by the use of power and politics.

2. *Role orientation*—the desire to be as rational and orderly as possible, organizational life being governed principally by considerations of rights, privileges, legality, and legitimacy.

3. *Task orientation*—the desire to get the job done and achieve results, organizational life being dictated mainly by what would facilitate task accomplishment.

4. *Person orientation*—the desire to serve the needs of the organization's members, organizational life being principally guided by considerations of what would best satisfy the members' needs.

Charles Handy categorized industries according to Roger Harrison's culture types and described what it was about these industries that led to the type of culture indicated.[11] Organizations rarely fall neatly into one of these four types of culture, so think about which culture type is *dominant* in your organization. As in the case of one's personal value system, it is the relative ordering of the values that distinguishes one culture type from another. The relative ordering is revealed when two values come into conflict.[12] For example, two organizations may be both role oriented and task oriented, but if the emphasis is on getting the job done even if some rules have to be ignored or roles altered, then task orientation is dominant (as is common in consulting firms, for example). However, if the emphasis is on following the rules and staying within the prescribed roles even if task performance suffers as a result, then role orientation is dominant (as is common in bureaucratic organizations, for example).

The organization Bob Drake joined was *power* oriented, but his personality[13] was not at all well suited to this type of culture (Figure 4). His personality was a much better fit in the culture of his prior organization, a government agency, where he had been very successful—and whose culture type was *role* orientation.

Which one of these four culture types best describes your organization? Which one of these four culture types is the best fit for you? Your answers to these two questions will indicate whether you are a misfit in the culture of your organization or not.

Figure 4 allows you to make a quick and useful assessment regarding culture misfit, but it does not reveal the *extent* of your misfit or the *specific*

Roger Harrison's Terminology[a]	• Power	• Role	• Task	• Person
Charles Handy's Illustrative Types of Firms[b]	• Small entrepreneurial firms • Investment banks • Brokerage houses	• Bureaucratic organizations • Insurance companies • Commercial banks	• Consulting firms • High-technology firms	• Professional groups (doctors, lawyers, etc.) • Universities • Research and development

[a]Harrison, R. (1972, May–June). Understanding your organization's character. *Harvard Business Review, 50*(3), 25–43.

[b]Adapted from Handy, C. (1978). *Gods of management.* London, United Kingdom: Souvenir Press.

Figure 4 Types of culture

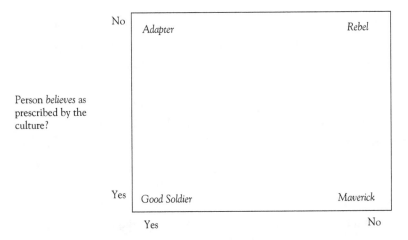

Figure 5 Culture Map

beliefs/values of your organization's culture. The Culture Map (Figure 5) can help you to do that.

Culture Map

Ask yourself two questions: (1) "Are your *beliefs* (including your evaluative beliefs, i.e., your values) congruent with your organization's culture?" and (2) "Do you *behave* as prescribed by the culture?" The answers to these two questions place you somewhere on the Culture Map, with its four corners labeled by the culture caricatures: *good soldier, adapter, maverick,* and *rebel.*

Good soldiers have the best fit with the culture because they believe and behave as prescribed by it. The intrinsic value of having this ideal fit may be one of the reasons they stay in the organization.

Adapters do not believe as prescribed by the culture but they conform to its cultural norms—that is, the expectations concerning appropriate behavior.[14] Adapters do as the culture prescribes because they look upon work as a job to be done in exchange for the extrinsic benefits (such as pay, status, and perks) or because they feel unable to deviate from the cultural norms.

Mavericks believe as prescribed by the culture but they violate the cultural norms. They may be accepted in the organization if they make valuable contributions. Mavericks cherish the cultural beliefs and values. Their quarrel is with the corresponding expectations concerning appropriate behavior—that is, the cultural norms, which they view as dysfunctional or inconsistent with the cultural beliefs and values.

Rebels have the worst fit of all, because they neither believe nor behave as prescribed by the culture. Rebels are tolerated if they make contributions that are *vital* to the organization. A rebel may also be tolerated because others in the organization have no choice in the matter—his or her formal position or political power may give the rebel enough clout to stay. One example is a leader seeking to change the cultural beliefs and behavior, and fundamentally transform the organization.

In general, the greater your distance from the good soldier location on the Culture Map, the worse is your fit with the organization's culture. Bob Drake was a rebel, the worse possible fit. He didn't survive because, although his contributions were needed, they were not seen as vital to the organization, and he did not have sufficient clout to flaunt the organizational beliefs/values and norms. Bob was not trying to be a reformer, but what if he had been? Or what if Bob had wanted to make it in the organization despite his terrible misfit with the culture? What could Bob have done differently?

Bob had at least two options, but he pursued neither. First, he could have tried to be more flexible by conforming to the cultural norms to become an adapter.[15] Although Bob would have found such conformity painful, it might have permitted him to survive in the organization long enough to make valued contributions, and perhaps earn sufficient credibility to allow him to become a rebel later on. Second, Bob might have concluded that his misfit with the culture was irreconcilable and left sooner.

How You Can Use the Culture Map

There are four ways in which you can use the Culture Map in Figure 5:

1. To understand your place in the organization's culture
    Since your position on the Culture Map has important implications for your survival and ability to contribute to the organization, it can be used to think about questions such as the following:
    Where am I located on the map? Why?
    If the current location is untenable, what are my alternatives?
    Where do I want to be on this map in the future?

2. To determine the positions of your boss and the other key players on the Culture Map
    Are your boss and the other key players located close to you or far away on the Culture Map? The greater the distance between you and another person on the Culture Map, the greater is your misfit with that person.

    Also think about the distribution of others in your organization on the Culture Map. For example, an organization with no mavericks or rebels is qualitatively different from one that accepts such nonconformity.

3. To better understand an organization's beliefs/values and norms
    To place yourself and others on the Culture Map, you have to think more clearly about its two dimensions—beliefs/values and norms. Used in this way, the map is a tool for understanding the organization's culture.

4. To think about what kind of culture you want to have
    Both organizational leaders and members can use the Culture Map to think about the culture they desire. A leader can ask: What are the beliefs/values and norms that I am trying to instill in this

organization? What should be the distribution of people on the Culture Map? An organizational member can ask: Is this the kind of culture I want to work in? Why? Can I do anything to try to change the distribution of people on the Culture Map?

Draw One Culture Map for Each Belief/Value and the Corresponding Norms

It is best to create *one* Culture Map for each belief/value and the corresponding norms. For example, Bob Drake was a rebel on the organization's most important cultural belief/value, that of cutthroat internal competition and the corresponding norms that encouraged beating your internal competitors at any cost. Drake neither believed nor behaved like this. But consider the organization's next most important belief/value of delivering promised results. Drake had bought into this belief/value but he was not willing to *behave* as prescribed by the culture (i.e., the norms concerning the use of any means at one's disposal, whether ethical or not, in order to deliver the promised results). On this belief/value he was a maverick, not a rebel.

Thus, the following steps are recommended for using the Culture Map:

1. List the top three beliefs/values of the organization's culture.
2. For the most important belief/value, what are the *corresponding norms*? Is there sufficient evidence to locate the individual on the Culture Map for this belief/value and the corresponding norms? If yes, note the location.
3. Repeat the procedure for the second most important belief/value and the corresponding norms.
4. Repeat the procedure for the third most important belief/value and the corresponding norms.

The individual may end up in roughly the same location on the Culture Map for the three most important cultural beliefs/values. But what if the individual's locations are widely dispersed on the map for the three most important beliefs/values? Then it is not very meaningful to talk about the person's overall location on the Culture Map. In such cases, it is best to refer to the individual's location on the map for a *particular* belief/value. For example, Drake was a rebel on the Culture Map for the belief/value of cutthroat internal competition, but he was a maverick for the belief/value of delivering promised results.

Summary

Key #1 to creating a positive impact for your organization and yourself is your fit with the key players and with the organization's culture. The better the fit, the easier it is for you to do your job well, and make other contributions to the organization, while creating positive outcomes for yourself.

Since misfits are common, Key #1 provides the concepts, frameworks, and tools you need to assess the extent of your misfit ("values gap"). If there is an *irreconcilable* misfit ("unbridgeable gap"), it is best to make plans to move on if you can. Other misfits need to be managed constructively (see Key #9).

While Key #1 is your fit with the key players and the culture of the *organization*, Key #2 is your fit with the *job*—specifically your job challenges in relation to your skills, your effort, and the support you require to do your job well.

KEY #2

Your Job Challenges Versus Your Skills, Effort, and Support

Your ability to create a positive impact for your organization and yourself also depends on your fit with the job, specifically your job challenges and whether or not you (1) have the necessary skills to address these challenges, (2) put in the required effort, and (3) receive adequate support to do your job (Figure 6). The bigger the misfit ("skills, effort, and support gap"), the more difficult it is for you to create a positive impact for your organization and for yourself.

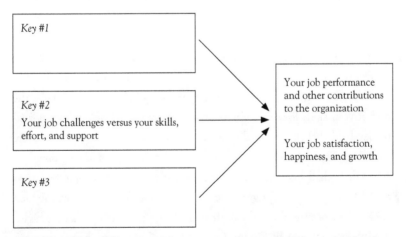

Figure 6 Your ability to create a positive impact for your organization and yourself depends on your job challenges in relation to your skills, your effort, and the support you receive to do your job

Research on "Flow"

For over 40 years, Professor Mihaly Csikszentmihalyi and his associates have conducted careful research on "flow"[1]—the deep sense of enjoyment one feels when one is immersed in what one is doing. When in flow, your sense of time is altered, you tend to forget yourself, and you feel a strong sense of being in control.

These researchers have studied thousands of people engaged in an amazing array of activities (including climbing mountains, playing chess, making pottery, and even operating on patients). The research subjects wore beepers as they went about their business and filled out a short questionnaire on what they were doing and how they felt each time they were beeped, which occurred randomly several times a day over several days.[2] The resulting research database of literally millions of observations is a unique accomplishment.

Flow Conditions

This stream of research has revealed the specific conditions that facilitate flow: clear goals, immediate feedback, and a balance between challenges and skills. The first two conditions, concerning goals and feedback, have long been emphasized in the literature on industrial psychology and human resource management because of their positive impact on job performance and personal development.[3] The third, a balance between challenges and skills, is receiving increasing attention in the literature on positive psychology.[4]

Figure 7, based on the work of Mihaly Csikszentmihalyi, asks two questions: (1) "How great are the challenges of your job?" and (2) "What is the level of your skills for dealing with these challenges?" People who reported low levels of challenges and skills in what they were doing when they were beeped in Csikszentmihalyi's research reported feeling *apathy* or *boredom*. When their challenges were low but their skills were high, people felt *relaxation*.[5] When their challenges were high but their skills were low, they felt *anxiety*. *Flow* occurred when both their challenges and their skills were high.[6]

The *comfort zone* in Figure 7 is not from Csikszentmihalyi's research but from my work in which people report feeling in the "comfort zone" when both challenges and skills are moderate. If you find yourself in this comfortable state, you need to raise your level of challenges and skills to experience flow.

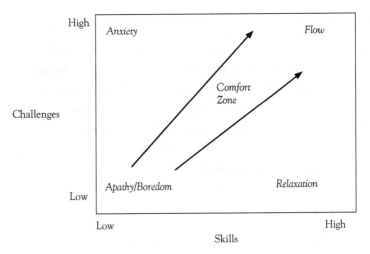

Figure 7 *Where are you on this map?*

Based on Csikszentmihalyi, M. (2003). *Good business: Leadership, flow and the making of meaning* (Fig. 1, p. 67). New York, NY: HarperCollins.

Flow and Job Performance

Do people in flow deliver high performance? Do those who feel anxiety because their job challenges exceed their skills perform poorly on the job? What happens when your skills exceed your job challenges? Will your resulting relaxation hurt your job performance?[7] These questions cannot be answered by the research on flow because it has focused on a person's subjective experience without examining his or her performance.[8] I have observed the following pattern, which I am now testing more rigorously in my research: If your skills are low but your job challenges are high, you will feel anxiety and your job performance will suffer (Figure 7). If your skills and your job challenges are both high, you are likely to experience flow and perform well. If your skills are high but your job challenges are low, you will feel relaxed and can deliver high performance in your job— provided you put in the necessary effort.[9]

With competition heating up around the world, the goal in today's organizations is to get outstanding or "A performance" in all jobs. The theory of this book is that your performance and other contributions will depend in part (Key #2) on whether or not you have the required skills, put in the necessary effort, and receive sufficient support to address your job challenges.

Your Job Challenges

There are three important sets of challenges in any job: technical challenges (related to specialization in the work to be done), business challenges (concerning the particulars of the industry and the business), and organizational challenges (associated with people and politics in the organization). Your job performance depends on whether you have the corresponding skills—technical skills, business skills, and people/political skills—to effectively address these challenges.

Your Skills

Howard Gardner defines intelligence as the ability to solve problems and describes multiple intelligences, including logical–mathematical, linguistic, spatial, and interpersonal.[10] Justin Menkes identifies three sets of cognitive skills that determine how well an executive performs: accomplishing tasks, self-evaluation, and working with other people—including the ability to recognize underlying agendas, understand multiple perspectives, and anticipate likely emotional reactions.[11] Emotional intelligence (EI) is now widely viewed to be just as important as IQ, if not more so. EI is the cluster of skills relating to the emotional side of life; for example, the ability to recognize and regulate our own emotions, to influence the emotions of others, and to self-motivate. As Daniel Goleman points out, IQ and technical skills are important, but EI is the *sine qua non* of leadership.[12]

Beyond the specific skills required to meet the challenges of a particular job and organization, today's "dual-focus"[13] workers—those who must manage work and personal/family life simultaneously because they do not have sufficient support at home—must possess a set of general competencies in order to be effective in today's work environment. These include the ability to deal with ambiguity and complexity, resilience and adaptability, emotional intelligence and relationship management skills, and communication skills, including the ability to negotiate and persuade others.

The Effort You Put In

Your performance also depends on whether you are motivated to put in the necessary effort, and if so, the quality of that effort. If you are doing the job primarily for its extrinsic rewards, you will put in the effort necessary to obtain these rewards. If, however, your primary motivation is intrinsic, there is no limit to the quantity and the quality of the effort you might put in, because the task itself is rewarding.[14]

Your motivation depends on your work orientation. Based on extensive study of a number of professions, the sociologist Robert Bellah and his associates[15] distinguish between three very different work orientations: *job*, *career*, and *calling*.

People for whom work is just a *job* (see Figure 8)[16] do it to satisfy their basic needs for security, money, power, and status, and the motivation is primarily extrinsic. Those who view their work as a *career* are also satisfying their needs for advancement and achievement, and their motivation is both extrinsic and intrinsic.[17]

In its original use, *calling* meant being "called" by God to do morally and socially significant work, but in its modern use the term has lost its religious connotation and has retained its meaning of doing work that makes a contribution to the wider world.[18] Those who view their work as a *calling* are seeking to contribute something of value beyond themselves—for example, serving a cause, a person, or an ideal.[19] Such self-transcendence[20] is closely linked to self-actualization and the motivation is primarily intrinsic.

The Power of Calling and What We Know About It

Abraham Maslow is best known for his hierarchy of needs, beginning with physiological and safety needs; extending through needs for love, the respect of others, self-esteem, advancement, achievement; and culminating

Work Orientation (Bellah)	Needs (Maslow)	Motivation
Job	Security, money, power, and status	Extrinsic
Career	Advancement and achievement	Extrinsic and intrinsic
Calling	Self-actualization	Intrinsic

Based on Ellsworth, R. (2002). *Leading with purpose* (p. 82). Stanford, CA: Stanford Business Books.

Figure 8 Job, career, and calling

in self-actualization or self-fulfillment.[21] In summarizing the findings of 30 years of research after the development of his hierarchy of needs, Maslow reached a profound conclusion that is not as widely known as his hierarchy: "Self-actualizing people are, without one single exception, involved in a cause outside their own skin, in something outside of themselves. They are devoted, working at something, something that is very precious to them—some calling or vocation in the old sense, the priestly sense."[22] Self-actualization is thus a *byproduct* of self-transcendence and cannot be achieved by directly seeking it.[23] If your work is your *calling*, you are more likely to achieve self-actualization not because you set out to get there but as a natural consequence of the goals you are pursuing. You are more likely to be in flow because, as Csikszentmihalyi points out, people who enjoy that optimal experience are pursuing goals that originate in a strongly directed purpose that is not self-seeking.[24] Such purpose-driven work gives greater meaning and significance to your life, and it allows you to focus your limited psychic energy on goals that you care about. The result is enjoyment, personal growth, and inner harmony.[25]

Empirical research by Amy Wrzesniewski and her colleagues reveals that people's orientations to their work fall along two orthogonal dimensions: (1) whether they view their work as a career or not and (2) whether they view it as a job *or* as a calling—people who view their work as a job tend *not* to also view it as a calling and vice versa.[26] Also, the same work can be a job for one person but a calling for another. Thus, it is not the design of the work[27] that determines the work orientation but rather how the person who is performing the work views it.

The behavior, attitudes, and emotions of people who view work as a calling are quite different from those who view work as a job or as a career. Research shows that people who pursue their work as a calling tend to put more time in at work, whether or not this time is compensated, report higher job and life satisfaction, and derive more satisfaction from work than from leisure activities and hobbies.[28]

How do people who view their work as a calling come to have this work orientation and can others acquire it? One possibility is that those with a calling orientation have sought out work that fulfilled their need to find meaning in their work.[29] One factor that seems to contribute to a calling orientation is good psychological health; traits such as optimism, mastery, and conscientiousness may be associated with viewing work as a calling. Research by Amy Wrzesniewski and Jane Dutton on "job crafting" offers insight into how people with different orientations toward their work may actually structure their work differently in ways that help to create or undermine meaning in their work. Through job crafting, one can realize a calling orientation by reshaping the task in ways that allow one to view the work as making a bigger contribution to the wider world.[30]

It may be that one has to learn how to do the job well before being able to undertake job crafting. Anecdotal evidence from work that my colleague Dick Ellsworth and I have been doing over the last 10 years with a financial services firm suggests that the typical new financial advisor (FA) joins the firm viewing it as a job. Those FAs who learn to do the job well and progress in the organization may come to see it as a rewarding career that can sustain them and their families. It is only later, typically 5 to 10 years after they begin, that some of the FAs begin to hear from their clients about how the financial advice given changed their clients' lives for the better, by enabling them to send their kids or grandkids to school, or by allowing them to retire with dignity. For these FAs, what was once a job and then a career becomes a calling to change people's financial lives for the better. These FAs no longer work to make money; they work to serve others, and money becomes a byproduct of a meaningful work life.

If you are a manager or plan to become one, what is your conception of management? I provoke the thinking of my MBA and executive students with the following statement: "If you are a bad painter, you create a bad painting. If you are a bad manager, you harm another human being. If you are a good manager, you can change a life for the better."

Those who consider management to be a noble profession—with the potential to improve people's economic and professional lives as well as their psychological well-being—may come to view their work as a calling, with a greater purpose than security, money, achievement, and advancement.

Whether you are a manager or not, do you view your work as a job, as a career, or as a calling? Your answer will influence not only your motivation and the quality of the effort you put into your work but also how you manage other people if you are responsible for any. Your work orientation thus affects your job performance as well as your job and life satisfaction, happiness at work, and personal growth.[31]

The Support You Receive to Do Your Job

Two sources of support are important. The first is the availability of sufficient[32] financial, human, and other resources to do your job, and the organizational support systems (such as education and training programs, high-performance work practices,[33] information and control systems, performance-management systems, etc.) to help you do your work. The latter are often taken for granted by those who have been with the enterprise for a while; their importance may be revealed only later when one moves to an enterprise that has systems that are either better or worse. For example, General Electric (GE) is famous for its robust support systems and many GE alumni came to fully appreciate the support they received from these systems only after they left GE.[34]

The second source of support[35] is your key players and others who are important to your survival and success (Exhibit 1, page 4). They can help to bring your work conditions into better alignment with the three flow conditions—job challenges that are in line with your skills, clear goals on which your performance will be judged, and valid and timely feedback on how you are performing your job.[36] The better your relationships with these people, the more they will support you on these and other important matters, including the crafting of your job to make it more meaningful for you.

Summary

Key #2 to creating a positive impact for you and your organization is your fit with the job, specifically your job challenges in relation to your skills, your effort, and the support you receive on your job. The bigger your "skills, effort, and support gap" the more difficult it will be for you to do the job well.

Every job has its technical, professional, and people/political challenges, and you need the appropriate skills to address these challenges. If your skills exceed the challenges, you will feel relaxation and have the ability to do your job extremely well; you will need to take on additional challenges to experience flow. If your skills fall short of the challenges, you will feel anxiety, but there is the opportunity to increase your skills to improve your job performance and experience flow.

You also need to put in the necessary effort, and the quantity and the quality of your effort will depend on whether you feel sufficient extrinsic and intrinsic motivation, which in turn depends on whether you see your work as a job, a career, or a calling.

The support you receive to do your job also matters. One important source of support is the availability of sufficient resources to do your job and the organizational systems to help you to do your work. A second vital source of support is your key players and others who are important to your survival and success; their emotional and task support will depend on the quality of your relationships with them. That is the subject we turn to next.

Art by Jeffery Schidlowsky

Build Bridges to Close Your Gaps

KEY #3

The Quality of Your Relationships With the Key Players and Others

Your ability to create a positive impact for your organization and yourself also depends on the quality of your relationships with the key players and the other people who are important to your survival and success (Figure 9).

These people's values may not be congruent with your values but—unless the misfit is *irreconcilable*—this should not prevent you from developing good working relationships with them. In fact, the worse your fit with them (Key #1), and the more support you need from them to do your job (Key #2), the more important it is for you to develop good working relationships with them.

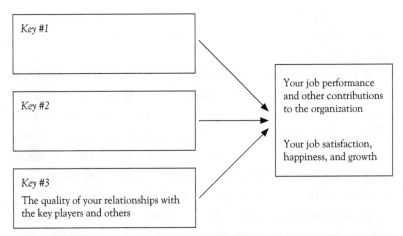

Figure 9 *Your ability to create a positive impact for your organization and yourself depends on the quality of your relationships with the key players and others*

Viewed in this light, the quality of your relationships with the key players and others is the master key that can enable you to bridge both the "values gap" on Key #1 and the "skills, effort, and support gap" on Key #2.

There are three critical ingredients for having good relationships with these people: (1) you are clear about their expectations of you and there is no agenda mismatch, (2) they trust you, and (3) you are able to influence them.[1] If you can influence others but they don't trust you, they will go along but resent it. Influence moves people in the direction you want; trust provides the lubrication that allows motion without friction. *Thus, even if you are clear about what the key players expect of you, high levels of one of the other ingredients—either trust or influence—will not produce good relationships without at least moderate levels of the other.*

Are You Clear About What Your Key Players and Others Expect of You? Is There an Agenda Mismatch?

Are you clear about what your key players and others who are important to your survival and success (Exhibit 1, page 4) expect of you regarding your job performance and other contributions?[2] What do they truly value? What are their expectations about how you will go about making these contributions? Some of their expectations may be explicit but others may be implicit or unconscious. The bundle of their expectations—both conscious and unconscious, short term and longer term—is their "agenda" for you.[3]

What are your own expectations about your job performance and other contributions you wish to make? Surprising as it may seem, research has shown that you may not be fully aware of what you are really trying to accomplish in your job. Your actual behavior on the job may reveal unconscious expectations about yourself of which you may not be aware.[4] Your bundle of expectations—both conscious and unconscious, short term and longer term—is your "agenda."

To build good relationships with your key players and others, you must be clear about your own agenda as well as their agendas for you. Agenda mismatches must be discovered and addressed; failure to do so is a major reason for poor relationships. For example, Bob Drake, the new manager, joined the company because his agenda was to become a line manager, and he expected the company to give him this opportunity. His boss's agenda, however, was to utilize Bob's analytical skills in a staff capacity. The agenda mismatch was never addressed, and it hurt Bob's relationship with his boss.

Do the Key Players and Others Trust You?

Trust describes a *relationship*, not a person. Others trust you to the extent that they feel assured that you will not take malevolent or arbitrary action. Their trust is based on how they perceive your character and competence.[5] Their judgments about your *character* are based on the following:

- *Integrity*—your basic honesty
- *Intentions*—your motives
- *Reliability*—the sense that you are consistent and predictable (no surprises)
- *Openness*—the sense that you are open with them in discussing problems
- *Discretion*—the assurance that you will not violate confidences or carelessly divulge sensitive information

Their judgments about your *competence* will be based on the following:

- *Specific competence*—the specialized knowledge and skill required to do your job
- *Interpersonal competence*—your skill in dealing with people and politics
- *Business sense*—your knowledge of the industry and your company's business

As the above list indicates, others assess you on a variety of bases: "Her integrity is not in question, but I don't trust her business judgment." "He is well intentioned, but his handling of people leaves a lot to be desired." Thus the key question is: in what areas and to what extent are you trusted by your key players and others who are important to your survival and success?

What happens if *you* do not trust some of these people? For example, you might not be open with them because you don't trust their integrity or their motives. They, in turn, do not trust you because they can see that you don't trust them, and a vicious circle spirals downward to lower levels of trust. If your evidence clearly indicates that one or more key players cannot be trusted, you may have no choice but to live with that and work on the other two aspects of your relationships with them—by clarifying agendas and increasing your ability to influence them.

Do You Have the Power to Influence the Key Players and Others?

Power is the *capacity* to affect the behavior and thinking of others. *Influence* is the *use* of power to affect the behavior and thinking of others. *Manipulation* is influence that others perceive as illegitimate, and it thus damages relationships. What is considered illegitimate depends on others' personal values, on the organization's culture, and on broader community values. For example, attempts to influence others by withholding relevant information—or influence attempts that do not provide others with the opportunity for free and informed choice—are generally perceived by others as manipulation.[6]

As with trust, power is a characteristic of a *relationship* rather than an attribute of an individual. Power also has several bases, which may be grouped into two major categories: *positional* bases of power, associated with your formal position in the organization; and *personal* bases of power, which derive from your personality, skills, resourcefulness, and other personal assets.[7]

The *positional* bases of power that derive from your formal *authority* include the following:

- Power to *structure* another's tasks or formal organizational relationships
- Power to *reward* and punish the other person
- Power to allocate or *control* resources valued by the other person
- Power to *direct* the other person

The *personal* bases of power include the following:

- Building a reputation as an *expert* in the eyes of the other person
- Fostering the other's conscious or unconscious *identification* with you
- Possessing personal *information* and resources valued by the other person
- Creating a sense of *obligation* in the other person
- Having the ability to *reduce the uncertainty* felt by the other person

These bases of power can be remembered by thinking about the five vowels of the English alphabet—A (for Authority)–E–I–O–U. The following are other bases of personal power:

- Having *charismatic* appeal in the eyes of the other person
- Being able to *persuade* the other person
- Being able to create perception of *common goals*
- Affecting the other's perception of *dependence* on self for resources and help

The bases of power, like the bases of trust, are differentiated. You may have the power to influence another in some areas but not in other areas, just as you may be trusted in some respects but not in other ways. This differentiation is an important feature of both trust and power, but for simplicity we will typically refer to trust and power in the aggregate.

The Limits to Formal Authority

In today's organizations, your formal authority—however great—is not sufficient for you to get the job done.[8] There are three main reasons for this. First, people are no longer awed by authority and are turned off by influence attempts based on it. If there is any doubt in your mind about this, how do *you* feel when your boss tells you to do something because he is the boss? Second, other than your subordinates, your key players do not report to you, so you cannot use your formal authority to influence them. Third, this is also true for many others you depend on to get your job done. The following simple exercise will help you to visualize and analyze this.

Take a piece of paper and draw your organization chart, with your name at the top. Add the positions of your direct subordinates, if you have any, and their subordinates, and so on until all the positions that you are responsible for are included on the organization chart. This is a map of your formal authority relationships.

Now make a list of the 10 people you depend on the *most* to get your job done and locate them on the chart—or off the chart if they do not report to you either directly or indirectly. Go ahead, take a few minutes and actually list these people by name and locate them on or off the chart.

A typical list would include your boss and others both inside and outside your organization. For example, a salesperson's most important customers would be among the 10 people the salesperson is most dependent on to get his or her job done, and they would not be located on his or her organization chart. How many of the 10 names on your list are people who report to you, either directly or indirectly? These are the ones you can influence with your formal authority. Let's call this number "N." How will you influence the others (10 minus N) who do not report to you but on whom you depend to get your job done?

I have conducted this exercise with managers from all over the world, and two patterns have emerged. First, N is *lower* for those who work nearer the boundaries of the organization—for example, sales people—because a lower number of their top 10 people report to them. Second, N is *lower* as one moves up in the hierarchy. For example, the typical CEO is most dependent on key customers, board members, investors, regulators, government officials, and others over whom he or she has no formal authority. So the people at the top who are considered to be so powerful (they *are* powerful relative to other people in the organization) are pitifully powerless to influence (by the use of formal authority) those on whom they are most dependent. Everyone, and especially those seeking to move up, must learn to rely less on formal authority and more on personal bases of power to influence others.

Building and Maintaining Good Relationships

As described later (Key #7), it takes 12 to 18 months to develop a good relationship. And a good relationship, once developed, can still easily sour. It is much harder to build a good relationship out of a poor one, but it can be done by destabilizing the poor relationship—either by taking action proactively or by seizing an opportunity to do things differently—and starting anew.[9] Relationship building, like cathedral building, is a slow process. Destruction of cathedrals, and of relationships, proceeds much faster.

Summary

The master key to creating a positive impact for your organization and yourself in any job, in any organization, is Key #3—the quality of your relationships with the key players and others who are important to your survival and success. This is because good relationships with these people can help you to overcome any misfits with them (Key #1), gain their support (Key #2), and as covered in the next chapter, develop your credibility with them (Key #4). It is the master key because it can help you to bridge both your "values gap" and your "skills, effort, and support gap."

There are three critical ingredients for having good relationships with these people: (1) you are clear about their expectations of you and there is no agenda mismatch, (2) they trust you, and (3) you have the power to influence them.

If the expectations and agendas of the key players and the others are inconsistent with your own agenda, you must take steps to get these differences resolved. If they don't trust you and/or if you do not have sufficient power to influence them, you can examine the specific bases of trust and power to see where improvement is possible.

KEY #4

Your Credibility in the Eyes of the Key Players and Others

Your credibility is your "brand image" in the organization and reflects your equity in the brand "You, Inc." Or, to use an analogy from finance, your credibility is your "credit rating" in the organization. Just as a good financial credit rating offers a cushion in managing your personal finances, your credibility gives you an organizational cushion to try new things and take necessary risks.

Credibility is in the eyes of the beholder. Your credibility with the key players and others who are important to your survival and success (Exhibit 1, page 4) is based on how they *perceive* your job performance and other contributions to the organization. Such perceptions are colored by how these people see your situation and also by the quality of your relationships with them.

Figure 10 shows how your job performance and other contributions are "refracted" through your "relationship lens" to influence your credibility. If your relationships with the key players and others are good, they will give you credit for good performance and other contributions, and this will build your credibility in their eyes; if not, they might attribute your positive results to your situation, or to other factors, with little or no improvement in your credibility with them.

Some people cannot accept the notion that good performance and other contributions may lead to no improvement in credibility because of poor relationships.[1] They view this as patently unfair and blame "organizational politics," as pointed out in the opening pages of this book. These people tend to become cynical rather than happy at work. But those who can see the underlying forces as inevitable facts of organizational life, and learn to deal with them, can build their credibility and become happy as well. Let us look more closely at Figure 10.

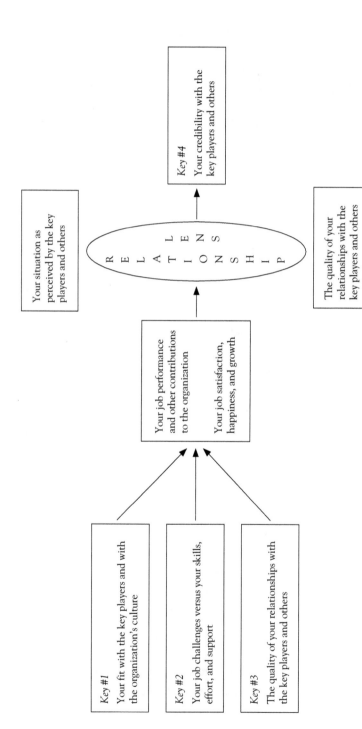

Figure 10 Your credibility with the key players and others depends on how they perceive your performance and other contributions to the organization

Your Job Performance and Other
Contributions to the Organization

Keys #1, #2, and #3 influence your job performance and other contributions you wish to make. To gain credibility (Key #4) with the key players and others, your performance and other contributions should be aimed at what *they* value. Credibility does not come from making contributions that you personally value, or contributions you think they should value, nor even contributions they say are valued. It comes from making contributions that they actually value.

What if your job is to make contributions that are important but not valued by your key players and others? Such was the case with the managers brought in to install information and control systems at Atlantic Engineering Company. When these managers succeeded, they gained credibility in the eyes of those who had recruited them for this task. However, these managers did not increase their credibility with others until these people began to value the role of systems at Atlantic.

Your Situation as Perceived by
the Key Players and Others

The perceptions of the key players and others are not based solely on your performance and other contributions, because the interdependency and uncertainty of organizational life makes it very difficult for these people to be sure what your performance and contribution really is. They will also rely on their perception of your situation in making this judgment. In extreme cases, they may attribute either positive or negative job performance and other contributions to what they regard as your favorable or unfavorable situation, with you getting little personal credit or blame.

The Quality of Your Relationships
With the Key Players and Others

The perceptions and attributions of the key players and others also depend on the quality of your relationships with them (Key #3). With better relationships, the perceptions and attributions are likely to be more favorable.

There are thus *two* important reasons why developing good relationships with the key players and others is at the heart of building your credibility with them: (1) the quality of your relationships with them affects the support you receive from them, which affects your ability to perform your job and make other contributions, and (2) the quality of your relationships with them affects the extent to which they give you credit for your performance and other contributions. In terms of equations, this can be represented as follows (f = function of):

1. Credibility = f (Relationships × Contributions). But,
2. Contributions = f (Relationships). Hence,
3. Credibility = f (Relationships Squared).

In short, if your relationships with the key players and others improve, your credibility with them will improve even more. On the other hand, if your relationships with them deteriorate, your credibility with them will deteriorate even more.

Thus, Key #3 (the quality of your relationships with the key players and others) is not only the master key that can help you to bridge your "values gap" on Key #1 and your "skills, effort, and support gap" on Key #2, it is the key that can turbocharge your credibility in the organization (Key #4) as well. It is thus more than a master key; it is the "magic wand."

Figure 10 makes clear why newcomers have little or no credibility. First, newcomers have had little time to develop good relationships with others in the organization. Second, they have had little opportunity to perform their job and make other contributions. Third, whatever credibility they have at the outset is based on background, expertise, and accomplishments in prior situations, which people in the new organization tend to discount. They usually adopt a wait-and-see attitude until they have an opportunity to work with the newcomer and see firsthand how well he or she can perform and contribute in *their* organization.

Perceptual Errors Versus Prejudice

Your credibility with the key players and others may be hurt because you are misperceived by them. Misperceptions may occur because of prejudice or perceptual errors.

We should note that you may also *gain* credibility because of perceptual errors or prejudice, as when you join an organization that looks favorably upon you because of your particular ethnic background, education, physical appearance, or other social characteristics. However, for ease of presentation, what follows assumes unfavorable perceptual errors or prejudice.

Perceptual Errors

Perceptual errors occur because there are limits to how much information people can absorb and comprehend in a given period of time. Stereotyping, for example, is a way of reducing information overload by simplifying one's world view.[2]

Those who are not prejudiced will change their perceptions of you with the passage of time, as more information is absorbed and comprehended. Initial inferences drawn from the signals thrown off by your surface characteristics (dress, grooming, language) and social characteristics (sex, race, age) will be modified as these people get to know you. First impressions are hard to change but others won't misperceive you forever.

The implications of this are that you should not be too quick to assume that others are prejudiced when you feel that you are being misperceived. You should manage the signals you throw off to the extent possible and give others some time to get to know you.

Al Hirsch, an individualistic and highly creative manager, was not willing to manage the signals he was throwing off. He insisted on driving high-priced European cars that the people in his company frowned on; they all drove modestly priced American cars. They recognized Al's contributions but resented his flamboyant driving habits. When I asked them why this was relevant ("Don't *contributions* count around here?"), I learned that the flashy cars gave Al an unfavorable image in their eyes. ("Of course contributions count; that is why he is well paid. But he thinks too much of himself.") Those who worked closely with Al didn't think he was a snob because they had sufficient opportunity to get to know him. But the flashy cars threw off signals that were misperceived by those who didn't have much personal contact with Al.

Did it matter? Yes, because it hurt Al's credibility in the company. People who did not know him well were less open and helpful to him *and to the people who reported to him.* When I mentioned this to Al, he said he was not going to "prostitute himself" for what he perceived as "*their* problem." In contrast, another manager, Roderick Smallwood, consciously dressed, groomed, spoke, and drove to conform to the culture in these areas because, in his words, "Those things are not important—I use my credibility where it counts, to make valued contributions." For example, on occasion Roderick was able to violate corporate policy and superiors' directives to complete licensing deals and introduce new products, which had then become winners in the marketplace.

These illustrations underscore three points. First, people in the organization with whom you do not have direct contact can misperceive you based on the signals you throw off, which is all they have to go by. Second, misperceptions can hurt your credibility. Third, if you stand out in an organization because of your sex, race, age, or other distinguishing social characteristics, you cannot do much about throwing off all kinds of signals that may be misperceived by others, a subject we turn to next.

Tokenism: A Special Case of Perceptual Error

This section is based on the work of Rosabeth Moss Kanter.[3] Tokenism is a special case of misperception that has important consequences for the organization and has a major impact on those directly affected by it.

These experiences apply to anyone who is numerically rare in a particular group—the few black people among a group of white people, the few white people among a group of black people, the few males among many females, the only woman among a group of men, the MBA among non-MBAs, the foreign-born among the native-born, the blind person among the sighted, the young person in a group of older persons, and so on.[4] The dynamics of tokenism are set in motion *not* by the social characteristic per se but because of certain perceptual tendencies that arise simply because of the way in which the few in a group tend to be seen in relation to the many.

To illustrate, consider the case of a female manager in an organization where all other managers are men. First, she may be overlooked, but if she is noticed she will get more attention than her male peers. Second, her presence makes the men more conscious of the social characteristic they share— being male—than they otherwise would be. Third, her presence may lead to invalid generalizations about all women and, conversely, stereotypes about women may be applied to her. Stereotyping is more difficult to do with the male managers because more examples of their type are available in the group. Their variety permits their individuality to be seen and makes over-simplified generalizations about male managers less likely.

These three perceptual tendencies, which Kanter has labeled *visibility*, *contrast*, and *stereotyping*, drive the dynamics of tokenism and lead to particular token responses or syndromes.[5] The basic forces at work and the types of responses to them are the same regardless of what specific social characteristic is involved, but the way in which these dynamics and token responses are manifested depends on the particular social characteristic and the situation. To illustrate, let us continue with the case of the lone female manager.

Visibility. Once noticed, she will get proportionately more attention than the typical male manager. Kanter describes three options she has for managing this perceptual tendency.

1. *Fear of visibility.* She can become socially invisible by avoiding public events and occasions that demand any kind of performance in the glare of publicity. She can quietly play background roles that keep the male managers in the forefront.
2. *Excessive trading on visibility.* She can take advantage of her visibility to get attention; but if this is perceived as overdone, she may alienate her peers. To maintain her visibility, she can attempt to discredit or exclude other women from joining the group, thus reinforcing the dynamics of tokenism and retaining her advantage.
3. *Walking a fine line between excessive trading on visibility and fear of visibility.* To create this delicate balance, she must be sensitive to the cultural and political forces at work. Public performance must be carefully orchestrated to minimize resentment and retaliation by peers and others. She must be able to survive organizational scrutiny and perform in the glare of publicity.

Contrast. Her presence makes the male managers more self-conscious of their social type (men), making it more difficult for her to become accepted into their culture. Kanter discusses three choices she has to deal with this perceptual tendency.

1. *Accept isolation.* She can become more an audience than a participant in the group's performance. This results in friendly but distant relations with the men.
2. *Join the dominants.* She can try to become an insider by showing that she believes and behaves like men. *If* this requires turning against her social category ("I am not like other women"), she must pay the psychic toll involved in doing this.
3. *Seek a creative synthesis.*[6] She can seek a course between isolation and insider by attempting a creative synthesis, accepting and acknowledging both the good and the bad in both male and female cultures. This creates more stress for her while the synthesis is being worked out but exacts a lighter psychic toll in the long run.

Stereotyping. Ironically, she is given visibility but denied individuality. Kanter mentions four caricatured roles into which she may be cast.

1. *Mother.* She may be stereotyped into the traditional nurturing maternal role—giving care and support to the men.
2. *Seductress.* She may be cast as a sex object, introducing an element of sexual competition and jealousy among the men.
3. *Pet.* She may be taken along as a symbol or mascot. Competent performance by her may be played down with the look-what-she-can-do-and-she-is-only-a-woman attitude.
4. *Iron Maiden.* She may be cast as a tough woman, be feared, and face abandonment.

Kanter outlines two options she has for dealing with such stereotyping:

1. *Accept the stereotype.* This saves her the time and awkwardness involved in trying to correct the mistaken impression. But it limits her range of expression and makes it difficult for her to demonstrate her competence and true potential. It also perpetuates the dynamics of tokenism.
2. *Fight the stereotype.* She can bend over backward not to exhibit any characteristics that reinforce the stereotype. She must steer a course between protection and abandonment by the men.

Whatever coping strategy is adopted, there is psychological stress for anyone in a token position. On the other hand, the opportunity is also there for improving one's competence and self-esteem by mastering these difficult situations. One general approach is to go it alone and bear the psychological cost. Another is to try to succeed and reduce that cost by forming an alliance with one or more others in a similar, or sympathetic, position.

It should be noted that the opportunity to personally interact with others is often the key to breaking down their misperceptions. As your direct dealings with others increase, their perceptual errors about you are likely to diminish. This is why it is possible to be perceived accurately in your work group but to be misperceived in the wider organization, as Al Hirsch was. It is also the reason that problems of misperception, and the opportunities to rectify them, continue throughout a career as you move from one job to the next and come into contact with people you have not interacted with before.

Heidi West suffered from being misperceived when she joined an organization as the only woman manager. She was stereotyped as "not tough enough." It took a year for people to realize that their stereotype of her ("not tough enough") was wrong. Over time, her credibility in the organization increased as her stereotyping by others diminished. In terms of an important cultural value, she was now seen as "caring but tough." The culture also shifted toward one of Heidi's personal values, "professionalism," and one of Heidi's values was modified from "analyze thoroughly" to "analyze but use intuition as well." These changes further contributed to her increased credibility. Heidi West advanced to become the only woman in the top management of the company. But even after this was achieved, she is now dealing with these issues all over again. Because of management turnover and a fresh crew from the outside, who are all male, she is now reliving some of the stereotyping she experienced when she first joined the company.

Prejudice

People who have strong, deep-seated beliefs about a particular sex, race, age group, and so on are not likely to change their beliefs quickly (see "Do personal beliefs and values change?" Key #1).[7] Indeed, their perceptions are likely to be controlled by their beliefs so as to reinforce their prejudice. Timothy Wilson (2002) points out as follows:

> When we meet somebody for the first time, we pigeonhole them according to their race or gender or age very quickly, without even knowing we are doing so. This process of automatic stereotyping is probably innate; we are prewired to fit people into categories. . . . No one is born with a particular stereotype about another group, but once we learn these stereotypes, usually from our immediate culture, we are inclined to apply them non-consciously, unintentionally, uncontrollably[,] and effortlessly. . . . (p. 53)

> It is becoming increasingly clear, however, that prejudice can exist at both an explicit level (people's conscious beliefs and feelings about other groups) and an implicit level (people's automatic evaluations of other groups of which they might not be aware). People can sincerely believe that they are not prejudiced and yet possess negative attitudes at an implicit level. (p. 133)

It is good to assume that others will not misperceive you once they get to know you better, but it is foolish to pretend that conscious or unconscious prejudice is absent when there is a consistent stream of behavior pointing to it. If prejudice is widespread in the organization, your only choices are to grin and bear it, or leave—unless you have sufficient credibility to create change (Key #10).

What to Do About "Jerks"?

As mentioned in the "Introduction," there is a danger of stereotyping people we don't like by calling them "jerks." But what if you are not falling into this trap and, based on a consistent pattern of behavior, feel that one or more of your key players or others are behaving like jerks? Robert Sutton offers some tips for stopping the inner jerk in us from coming out, and also for surviving the nasty behavior of others.[8]

One of the things you can look for is how *other* people, especially peers and superiors, feel about those who are behaving like jerks. Do they see what you see? If so, do they feel as you do? If they see and feel as you do, why do they tolerate this behavior? Is everyone aware of today's tough labor laws, at least in the United States, which can be invoked to counter discrimination and harassment in the workplace? The U.S. courts, particularly in California, have interpreted the laws very broadly to bar not just overt sexual or racial discrimination but also actions that discriminate by creating or tolerating a hostile work environment. But if those who are behaving like jerks are not creating a discriminatory environment in violation of any particular laws,[9] and since it makes no sense to talk about building good relationships and developing credibility with people who are behaving in this way, it may be best to find a better place to work if this is a chronic problem that you feel will not be fixed or is not worth your time and effort to fix.

Summary

Key #4 is your credibility in the eyes of the key players and others who are important to your survival and success. It depends on how these people *perceive* your performance and other contributions, which in turn depends on the quality of your relationships with them (Figure 10).

Key #4 opens the door for you to undertake new or politically risky initiatives, because the key players and others will cut some slack for you if things go wrong and even run interference if you have sufficient credibility with them.

Your credibility with the key players and others may be hurt because they misperceive you; tokenism is an important case of misperception. You should manage the signals you throw off to the greatest extent possible and give others some time to correct their misperceptions. But prejudice, whether conscious or unconscious, will not change so easily, and must be recognized for what it is and dealt with accordingly.

Four keys to creating a positive impact for your organization and for yourself have been covered in Part I. Attention now turns, in Part II, to those occasions when you are changing jobs within your organization, or leaving one enterprise to join another. These are times of great danger. But as the strong connection between danger and opportunity in the Chinese character for crisis (危机)[10] reminds us, these are also times of great opportunity—to choose a new job and organization wisely, and to enter into it smartly.

PART II

Determine Your "Values Gap" and Your "Skills, Effort, and Support Gap" *Before* Accepting a New Job

Are you changing jobs within the same organization? If so, there is a risk that you might fail. And the chance of failure is higher if you are joining a new organization because, per Key #4, you have little or no credibility in a new organization, regardless of your prior performance, contributions, and credibility.

The good news is that it is possible to avoid failure and create a positive impact for your organization and for yourself instead, by properly assessing yourself in relation to a new job and organization *before* accepting their offer (Key #5). It helps to interview smartly and avoid recruiting traps (Key #6).

Bob Drake thought he understood himself well and was clear about what he wanted when he accepted a company's offer. However, he later concluded that he was wrong about this.[1] He had failed to anticipate his culture misfit, which turned out to be irreconcilable, because he had ignored several early warning signs during the recruiting process. Bob was also convinced that he had been seduced by the company's extremely high salary offer and the tempting promise, which he felt they had not kept, of a line management position. He also concluded that he had seduced himself by not thinking more clearly about his agenda, that is, about what he really wanted in joining the company. The money and the opportunity had blinded him to other important personal values—professionalism and team play, in particular—which he had taken for granted. Bob learned from his mistakes, recruited smartly for the next job, and was able to help both himself and his next organization.

Art by Jeffery Schidlowsky

Determine What Your Gaps Are BEFORE You Accept a New Job

KEY #5

What You Need to Know *Before* You Accept a New Job

Prior to accepting a new job, you need to learn as much as possible about your fit with the key players and with the organization's culture (your "values gap" on Key #1); your job challenges in relation to your skills, your effort, and the support you will receive in your new job (your "skills, effort, and support gap" on Key #2); and the likely quality of your relationships (Key #3) with your key players and others (Exhibit 1, page 4), which is the "magic wand" that can help you to bridge both your "values gap" and your "skills, effort, and support gap" and turbocharge your credibility in the organization (Key #4).

You may have some incoming credibility with your boss or a few others who are pulling for you when you are hired, but it is safe to assume that your credibility in the new organization (Key #4) will be low to zero, no matter how great they say you are when you join.

Let us begin with what you need to know about *yourself*—your values, your skills, and your agenda. What you need to know about the new *job* and *organization* is considered later.

What Are Your Values, Your Skills, and Your Agenda?

"Know thyself," the philosophers tell us, but self-knowledge is not easily obtained. Two basic methods for learning about self are available: (1) self-insight from questionnaires and tests and (2) self-reflection based on personal experience. We will review these two approaches and then consider other work that throws additional light on this subject.

Gain Self-Insight From Questionnaires and Tests

Vocational counseling and assessment centers may be used for insight into your values and skills.[1] Vocational counseling provides systematic testing on a wide range of individual characteristics and the opportunity to analyze and interpret the results with professional staff assistance. Assessment centers use in-basket exercises, management games, role-playing simulations, leaderless group discussions, and oral and written presentations to arrive at their conclusions.[2] All such tests have their limitations and do not yield definitive answers.[3] Rather, they provide an opportunity for self-reflection and are sensitizing aids in the quest for self-insight.[4]

Your agenda is your bundle of expectations—whether you are conscious of them or not—about what you want to accomplish in the organization in the short term and in the long term. People are *not* fully aware of their own agendas, as discussed in Key #3, but a small group exercise can help to reveal them.[5] Each person in the group first writes down what he or she believes is a personal agenda. Next, each one is probed and queried by others in the group to better understand one's written agenda. Such cross-examination can lead to a much deeper understanding of your agenda because it forces you to make explicit what may have been implicit or subconscious.

Engage in Self-Reflection Based on Personal Experience

Personal experience is a great teacher if one is willing to learn from it.[6] Unfortunately, the human tendency to indulge in self-justification and rationalization makes this learning difficult by encouraging us to see things as we would prefer to see them rather than in perspective. For example, when the going is bad, we tend to take comfort by rationalizing poor outcomes and attributing them to causes other than ourselves.[7] Consider the following case.

One new manager, Jerry Rowland, did a poor job in a rather "hostile culture," as he called it, and was fired 3 months after joining the organization. He did not reflect on what really happened; nor did he learn from the experience. There were, in fact, several "red flags" that Jerry hadn't attended to during recruitment and entry, but Jerry proceeded to convince himself and persuade others that the company he had joined was crazy: "Boy, you should have seen those guys—they were really weird."

Jerry didn't learn much from his experience because he took no personal responsibility for his actions. He failed in two subsequent jobs but continued to look outward, and never inward, for his answers.

In contrast, Bob Drake took personal responsibility for his failure and learned that his values were ordered differently than he had thought. Money and line management opportunity were less important; a cooperative and professional working environment was more important to him than he had realized. Bob's insight led him to take some steps to remedy his situation. He sold his high-priced home and moved into a more modestly priced one to reduce his dependence on his high income, and he looked for a company in which he would have a much better fit with the key players and with the organization's culture. He did very well in his next job.

We can also fail to learn from experience when things are going extremely well because we take personal credit for positive outcomes. For example, the top management of one large, highly profitable company became afflicted over the years with the "golden touch" syndrome. ("We can't go wrong. Anything we touch turns to gold.") They explained their enviable financial record largely in terms of their management talent, discounting the more important near-monopoly position their major product lines had enjoyed because of patent protection. These product lines had been developed by the *prior* management generation, who had since departed. When competition that had been waiting in the wings finally came, the company's fortunes plummeted. The golden position they had inherited had lulled them into complacency and arrogance.[8]

In sharp contrast, the managers of another company that enjoyed the same kind of market dominance and financial success were more self-critical. When people inside and outside the company complimented them on their spectacular success, these managers acknowledged they had a good team that worked hard but would include caveats: "We are fortunate to have products and resources that our competition hasn't got," and "We make our share of mistakes too, but we try to learn from them." Depending on the circumstances, one or more war stories would follow to make the point that they were fallible and had to keep learning. These managers avoided the normal human tendency to take all the credit when they were successful. They continued to stay on top and the company has remained an industry leader.

The lesson to be learned is this: When things are going well and you are congratulating yourself on a job well done, you should also ask yourself, "What did *others* contribute to make me successful? Did luck play a role in my success?" When the going is not so good, the question to ask is, "To what extent am *I* a part of the problem?" Keeping yourself honest in this way will enable you to maintain a frame of mind that increases your chances of gaining insight from your personal experience.

Much can also be learned by reflecting on your past experience and asking questions such as the following[9]:

- In what previous jobs and working conditions have I been most productive? Most happy?
- What are the three or four previous occasions when things really didn't go as well as I had expected? What did I learn when I felt disappointment[10] or surprise?
- How have I responded to authority figures in the past?
- What kinds of people do I most like to work with? Least like to work with? Why?

The list can go on, but the point is that your own experience contains a wealth of relevant information that can be activated to good use if you can look at it objectively, by discounting the normal human tendency to rationalize and self-justify in defense of ego.

You can use the template for self-reflection in Appendix 1 to analyze your current or a prior situation at work using the 10 keys that are the focus of this book. A model paper that illustrates how the template can be used for this purpose is included in Appendix 1. The insights that such a disciplined self-examination can yield may help you to improve your job performance, job satisfaction, happiness at work, and personal and professional growth.

Learn From Recent Work on Self-Knowledge

Recent work throws new light on why self-knowledge is so difficult to obtain. It also shows how to go beyond self-assessments and learning from experience to understand ourselves better by observing our own behavior.

Based on a study of people who changed careers, Herminia Ibarra (2004) found that "knowing yourself" turns out to be the prize at the end of the journey rather than light at the beginning.[11] She points out as follows:

> Knowing, in theory, comes from self-reflection, in solitary introspection or with the help of standardized questionnaires and certified professionals. Once we have understood our temperaments, needs, competencies[,] and core values, we can go out and find a job or organization that matches. . . .
>
> But career change doesn't follow the conventional method. We learn who we are—in practice, not in theory—by testing reality, not by looking inside. We discover the true possibilities by *doing*— trying out new activities, reaching out to new groups, finding new role models, and reworking our story as we tell it to those around us. (pp. xi–xii)

Ibarra's conclusions are consistent with what we are learning about the unconscious mind. Neuroscience and psychological research on what people say versus what they actually do indicates that there appears to be a great deal about ourselves that we cannot know directly, even with our most painstaking introspection.[12] Timothy Wilson (2002) explains what follows:

> It can thus be fruitless to try to examine the adaptive unconscious by looking inward. It is often better to *deduce* the nature of our hidden minds by looking outward at our behavior and how others react to us, and coming up with a good narrative. In essence, we must be like biographers of our own lives, distilling our behavior and feelings into a meaningful and effective narrative. (p. 16)

We learn about the true nature of our personalities and how we really feel by observing what we do. Strange as it may seem, when trying to decide what is in our hearts and minds, we are in no better a position than a stranger who observes us from the outside.[13]

What You Need to Know About the Organization

Prior to accepting a job offer, every effort should be made to discover if you will have an *irreconcilable* misfit with the key players or with the organization's culture. You also need to find out as much as possible about the challenges of your job, and about the expectations and agendas of your key players and others who are important to your survival and success.

It may not be appropriate to *directly* question the people in the organization about these matters, because this might offend them or hurt you. Use your judgment and instincts to decide what to ask people directly and what to find out indirectly—for example, by observing people's behavior. Presented below are 20 questions you should *think about* but not necessarily ask. These questions can be used in the following ways:

- To keep track of what you know about your organization and what remains to be understood
- For sensitizing yourself to important questions in preparation for an upcoming visit to an organization and/or interviews with its representatives
- To ask whether you are subconsciously not exploring certain questions because of the fear that you will find unfavorable information that might be difficult to deal with

Twenty questions may seem to be too many, but insight comes from probing the same phenomenon in different ways rather than by looking for a correct answer with a few quick questions.

Twenty Questions to Think About (but Not Necessarily to Ask Directly) to Understand Your Organization

The term *organization* refers to both the corporation as a whole and the subunit (such as the department or division) in which you will be working.

Your Organization and Its Culture

1. What does the organization stand for? What is its purpose and mission?

The questions seek to understand why the organization exists and what its highest value is.

2. What kind of person is most respected in this organization? What is considered heroic?

   These questions also get at what is most valued in the organization.

3. What is viewed as punishment in this organization? What kinds of mistakes are not forgiven?[14]

   This is the other side of the coin revealed by the previous question. It gets at values that are counterculture.

4. What company folklore, rituals, symbols, and ceremonies best reveal the essential character of the organization?

   This is an attempt to understand the important shared beliefs and values by examining the various cultural sayings, doings, feelings, and artifacts.[15]

5. Pretend the organization is a person. How would you describe this person?[16]

   This is another way to tap into the culture of the organization, by personalizing it.

6. What are the important dos and don'ts in this organization?

   The question is intended to tap the organization's norms in such areas as dress, lifestyle, areas to live, places to be seen, whom to associate with, whom not to criticize in public, hours of work, what to say and do, and how to deal with others.

7. Who were the founders and others who built this organization? The answers should reveal their backgrounds and accomplishments, and may suggest what is really valued by the organization.

Your Job Challenges and Available Support

Technical, Business, and Other Challenges

8. What are the biggest hurdles that you have to overcome to do your job well?

   These hurdles could be technical, business, logistical, interpersonal, or political. ("Who are the likely adversaries or saboteurs?") The assessment here should consider *what* it will take and *how long* it will take to overcome these hurdles relative to the time available to get the job done.

9. What important sources of support are potentially available to you for getting the job done?

Here the attempt is to understand the technical, business, logistical, interpersonal, and political sources of support that are potentially available to help you to get the job done. The assessment should cover what these sources are and how long it will take to tap them, relative to the time available to get the job done.

People/Political Challenges

10. What are the people here like to work with? Why?[17]

The question probes for a general understanding of the personalities of the people in the organization.

11. Who are the key individuals and groups you will have to persuade? How does one go about selling a new idea in this organization?

The attempt here is to understand how responsive the organization is to new ideas, and to identify powerful individuals and important political camps that you have to work with to get new ideas implemented.

12. What are the important strategies and tactics for getting things done in the organization?

The question probes for an understanding of the informal workings of the organization, as well as the political games that will facilitate or hinder your ability to get things done within the organization.

13. Is there a possibility of becoming stereotyped in this organization? What is the status and progression of those who are similarly stereotyped?

The attempt here is to examine whether or not your particular background characteristics (age, sex, ethnic heritage, education) are likely to lead to stereotyping.[18] If they are, what will be the impact of this on your ability to get things done? Some knowledge of the success of others with similar background characteristics can provide valuable clues about what it will take for you to succeed in the organization.

You must be careful not to jump to conclusions on the basis of simple comparisons, particularly with only one or two other individuals. Your survival and success in an organization are influenced by many factors; explanations based on stereotyping alone can become self-fulfilling prophecies.[19] On the other hand, stereotyping does occur, and its consequences may be significant. Pretending or hoping it doesn't exist is also dangerous. Balanced assessment requires astute observation and careful, objective reasoning from evidence.

Your Key Players and Others Who Are Important to Your Survival and Success

Identify these people (Exhibit 1, page 4) and ask the following questions about them:

14. Do you like your prospective boss? Who are the other key players? Do you like them? What will your boss and the other key players like to work with?

    Their personalities, styles, beliefs, and values will have an important influence on your survival and success.[20]

15. Who are the others who will be important to your survival and success? Their personalities, styles, beliefs, and values will also have an influence on your survival and success.

The Expectations and Agendas of the Key Players and Others

It may prove difficult to decipher the expectations and agendas of your key players and others. Unconscious expectations that they have of you may not surface until you violate them, and by then it may be too late. Thinking about the following questions can help you to sniff out what may be consciously or unconsciously concealed from you.

16. Where are the individuals now who previously held the job for which you are being recruited? Why did they move on?

    If there has been turnover in your job or in similar positions, it is important to understand why these people moved on. If there were "recruiting mistakes," why did they occur? Why were these mistakes not anticipated during subsequent recruiting? Attempting to make sense of how others who started out in a position similar to yours progressed can also reveal the organization's view of your job, and how easy or difficult it is to change jobs or move from one functional area to another within the organization.

17. Why do the prospective boss and other sponsors and supporters want to hire you? What do they value most about you?

   This line of thinking is directed at the question of what makes you particularly attractive to them—your background, personality, values, training, talent, skills, and so on. Of greatest interest are assumptions and expectations that they will not or cannot communicate.

18. Are bait-and-switch, bait-and-keep, or bait-and-eat techniques being used to hire you?

   The *bait-and-switch* technique lures you into a position you find attractive and then switches you to a job more favorable for the organization. *Bait-and-keep* gets you into a job that is not very attractive by promising you a switch to another job later on, but then keeps you in your job by various means (e.g., by using salary raises or stock options as "golden handcuffs"). *Bait-and-eat* lures you into the organization because your talents and skills are desperately needed, knowing that you may not survive but will contribute what is badly needed.

Criteria for Assessing Performance and Other Valued Contributions

19. What are the spotlight measures of performance and other valued contributions? What are the spotlight rewards and punishments?

   The question attempts to tap the performance and other contribution measures most keenly watched, and the rewards commanding the greatest attention within the organization.[21]

20. What does it take to do well in this organization? How are good people recognized?

   In addition to the kind of performance that is important, the question may reveal particular background or personality characteristics that the organization considers desirable.[22] Is it a fast-track organization for MBAs? Is it an engineer's world? Does marketing dominate?

Summary

You need to know as much as possible about the keys to creating a positive impact for your organization and yourself (Keys #1 to #4, Part I) *before* you accept a new job. Key #5 shows you how to gain self-knowledge about your personal values, skills, and agenda as well as insight into the job and the organization you are considering joining.

When interviewing for a new job, every effort should be made to discover if you will have an *irreconcilable* misfit (an unbridgeable "values gap") with the key players or with the organization's culture. To do so, you need to go beyond self-assessments and learning from experience to understand yourself better—by observing your own behavior. You also need to find out as much as possible about the challenges of your job, and about the expectations and agendas of your prospective key players and others who will be important to your survival and success.

However, what you would *like to* know about a new job and organization must be tempered by what you *can* know, given the realities of recruiting and the difficulties encountered when interviewing for a new job. These realities and difficulties, and how to address them, are the subject of Key #6.

Art by Jeffery Schidlowsky

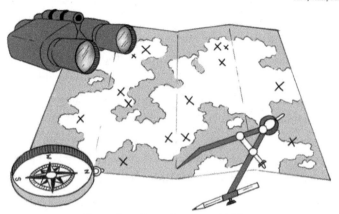

Interview Smartly to Avoid Traps

KEY #6

Interview Smartly to Avoid Recruiting Traps

To avoid an irreconcilable misfit (an "unbridgeable gap") with the key players and with the organization's culture, and to increase the chances of being successful after joining a new organization, you need to understand yourself and assess the new job and organization as best you can *prior to* accepting their offer (Key #5). Unfortunately, several difficulties in the recruiting process can derail this effort.

Key #6 shows you how to overcome these difficulties by interviewing smartly and probing carefully during the actual recruiting. What the critical questions are and whether you should ask them directly will be considered. Several subtle traps that plague the recruiting process will be described. Suggestions for coping with these traps and invisible dangers will be made.

What Are the Critical Questions to Be Answered *Prior* to Accepting a Job Offer?

As a guide to making information-gathering plans during recruiting, you should review the list of questions to think about (Key #5) and ask yourself: In light of my circumstances and preferences, what questions are absolutely essential to answer before making the decision to join? These key questions become a starting point in the quest for relevant information; other questions can be answered later on, even after starting in the new job.

When collecting information, what data would be relatively easy to get and also valuable to have? Knowing this helps to prioritize the questions that must be answered. In general, it makes sense to ask valuable questions on which valid data are readily available before venturing into other important but more sensitive areas.

Observe What You Cannot Ask

Many important questions concern matters that the people who are interviewing you cannot or will not discuss openly with you—for example, questions concerning the organization's taboos, secrets, personalities, and politics. Further, your manner of asking questions might be viewed as too direct, and hence may not be well received. This trap is less commonly recognized than the well-known issues of personal grooming, dress, and presentation of self. The trap can be avoided by asking as many questions as possible with *your eyes*—that is, by observing such details as these[1]:

- Use of space (office location, office space, where people live, etc.)
- Use of time (actual working hours, punctuality, tempo, etc.)
- Use of things (dress, opulent versus Spartan furnishings, symbols, logos, etc.)
- Use of language (often repeated words and phrases, jargon, etc.)
- Use of body language (expressions, gestures that affect the importance of what is said)

Asking questions with your eyes includes noticing and reflecting on the significance of people, places, and things *not* seen as well as those read about and observed:

- Why were certain people not included on the interview list? (Why were prospective peers not included?)
- Why were certain places not shown (such as one's prospective office location or office space)?
- Why was certain information not revealed? (Turnover was indicated, but actual names of people who left or transferred out were never revealed.)

Break the Language Code

If you begin by observing carefully and confining the verbal questions to those that are relatively nonthreatening, later verbal questioning can make use of the knowledge gleaned from observation. This approach can be extremely useful in helping you to deal with an important dilemma: The significance of the words used by the people in an organization may not become apparent until its language code is broken, but it is hard to decode without some understanding of the organization.

Bob Drake, for example, realized only later that he had not really understood the underlying significance of several phrases used by company executives recruiting him: "We play to win"; "This is a rough place but a fun place"; and "You will have to fight to get your points across." Given his background as a star college basketball player, Bob thought that *team* play and winning as a *team* were being alluded to. What was being communicated, however, was the importance of winning *against* team members and competition *within* the team.

Unfortunately, such clues may be obvious only in retrospect after starting a new job, when you have gained additional exposure and insight into the organization. Nonetheless, your chances of unraveling the language code increase if you have a preliminary understanding of the people in the organization and probe judiciously to try to understand the underlying *meaning* of the words and phrases that people use.

For example, Bob Drake was aware that turnover at his level had been high. When he asked about this, he was told that "only strong managers survive here, weak ones don't cut it." Bob might have tried diplomatically to get the names of one or two of those who couldn't cut it to find out why. A company may be reluctant to divulge such information (especially the names of those who may be critical of the organization), but the discovery of such reluctance is itself an important piece of information. There is a real danger that the recruit may get biased information from a malcontent who is no longer with the organization. However, much can be learned from those who have left the organization if one discounts for their biases.

Even without being able to contact one of those who had left, Bob Drake might have reflected on why turnover was so high relative to the company's industry and tried to find out what people in the culture meant by "strong" managers versus those who were "weak" and unable to "cut it." He might also have thought about and perhaps asked: "Whom are you playing *against*?"; "Why is it a *rough* place?"; "What do you mean by having to *fight* to get your point across?"; or "Fight with *whom*?"

Questions to Ask: What, When, How, and to Whom?

In deciding *what* questions to ask, *when* and *how* to ask them, and *whom* to ask, you must think about your bargaining position vis-à-vis the organization in general and the interviewer in particular. An applicant in a relatively strong bargaining position may be more comfortable asking sensitive questions than someone in a weaker position would be. People with more interpersonal competence and good interviewing skills may be able to ask questions that others should avoid asking. With these caveats in mind, there are four types of questions—encompassing increasing levels of boldness—that you can ask to probe more deeply into areas where you are not getting satisfactory answers:

1. *Easy questions.* These questions evoke an apple-pie-and-motherhood answer. An example is "What is the future here for a person like me?" Such questions are good for filling time and leave the door open for respondents to answer as frankly as they like. These questions could also lead to more important areas, depending on the willingness of the respondent to be helpful and your ability to understand the underlying meaning of what is said.

2. *Sensing questions.* These take a position based on your sense of the situation and invite the respondent either to agree or disagree—for example, a question that begins, "From my day here, my sense is that. . . . Is this correct?" These questions let the respondent know that you have an opinion on the subject, however incomplete and tentative, making it difficult for the respondent to give you a vague answer.

3. *Dramatic questions.* These are more provocative versions of the sensing questions. Here you dramatize some knowledge of the situation, inviting the respondent to tone it down to reality: "Everything appears *perfect* around here . . . ," to which the answer might be, "That's great to hear, but let me tell you something. . . . "

4. *Challenging questions.* These questions show the greatest confidence in your knowledge of the situation, making it very difficult for the respondent to give you a vague answer—for example, "All companies I know experience some turnover of newcomers for a variety of reasons. How many recent hires have left from here?" Implicit in this

question is the presumption that one aspect of organizational reality is a tendency for newcomers to leave for a variety of reasons, which the respondent must either accept or challenge.

The four types of questions can be helpful, but you must ultimately trust your judgment and feelings about what is appropriate to ask and whether you feel comfortable asking it.

Next to consider are the subtle dangers that arise from *interactions* between you and the organization. The organization directly controls some of these traps, but you are in control of the others. It is beneficial for both sides to be aware of these traps because they benefit neither the organization nor you.[2]

Recruiting Traps Under the Organization's Control

Organizational Oversell

Since a company is trying to attract the best qualified candidates, there are strong incentives to oversell the organization by accentuating its positive features and deemphasizing the negatives.[3] The "golden future" syndrome is one way of steering the interview, by playing up the hoped-for future benefits and downplaying current realities. This overselling can be hyped up to the point that you will have a totally unrealistic or distorted view of the company, job, and your prospects in it.

Organizational Seduction

A more subtle but powerful organizational technique of influencing you is seduction.[4] Whereas applicants are generally aware of the games of overselling just mentioned and attempt to discount for them, they are less conscious of organizational seduction, which persuades you to accept a position without being informed of negative factors that might have prevented you from joining. The technique of organizational seduction involves three steps:

1. They make you an extremely tempting salary offer, say 50 percent above the highest offer you are considering.

2. They bathe you in flattery, with statements such as "We look only at the best, and you are the best among the best."

3. They give you the appearance of free choice, with statements such as "We are in no rush. Take as long as you want to make a decision." This is a shrewd step, because your perception of *choice* in making your decision is essential to securing your real commitment to it.[5]

What is so wrong about this process? Can an organization be faulted for making you a very attractive offer, for flattering you, and for giving you plenty of time for a decision?

If the flattery represents the facts of the case as honestly perceived by a company's representatives, nothing is wrong about this process—*unless* important information concerning the organization's real values or agenda for you are consciously withheld because such disclosure might cause you to refuse the offer. If the organization honestly discloses its real intentions and other relevant information, the three steps outlined above are a model for gaining your genuine commitment and deserves to be applauded.

To the contrary, Bob Drake came to realize that the company had seduced him. Their real agenda for Bob was to use his analytical talent in a staff capacity longer than he had been told. Since Bob knew the offer was extremely attractive and had noted the excessive flattery, he might have asked himself, "It's good to hear this, but am I really that great? Why does this company think so? Why does this organization want me so badly? What is the organization's agenda, especially in the short term? Are bait-and-switch, bait-and-keep, or bait-and-eat techniques likely possibilities?" (Question 18, Key #5). "Is their agenda consistent with my own? Will I be required to operate in a way that violates any of my personal values?"

Organizational seduction may also be involved when you are being recruited for a new job or a special assignment within the same enterprise. A senior manager, Thom Sailer, recruited John Hastings, a middle manager from another part of the company, with an offer John couldn't refuse. John was given a chance to be Thom's special assistant for a year as a stepping-stone to senior line management. John was away at an advanced management training program at the time and felt flattered that Thom, who was highly regarded in the company, had taken the trouble to visit him to make the offer in person. Thom needed help in implementing new information systems in his group and told John he could make an important contribution to the company.

Thom made passing reference to John's first assignment, which was to be a live case study of a "human behavior" problem. John accepted the offer without further investigation. He learned only later that the case study was an intense interpersonal conflict that Thom was having with a powerful peer. The offer had led John into what turned out to be an impossible assignment—mediating a conflict between two powerful superiors. Assignment seduction was involved because the "human behavior" problem was clearly Thom's highest priority in recruiting John, but Thom withheld the critical details from John at the time.

If the organizational seduction techniques of a tempting offer, flattery, and plenty of time to decide are apparent, you must probe further to determine what the organization's real agenda for you is.

Homosocial Reproduction[6]

People have a tendency to hire and select others in their own image. The candidates chosen are perceived to be "my kind of person" or "our type." Comparisons are made more or less consciously on the basis of such surface similarities as age, sex, ethnic background, social class, and education.[7] The prevalence of these surface similarities in a prospective organization indicates a strong possibility that homosocial reproduction is at work.

This tendency exists because of the uncertainties of organizational life, and the necessity of coping with them places a premium on mutual trust. It drives people to seek recruits who seem to resemble themselves and to avoid others who are perceived as different. The greater the uncertainty, the stronger is the tendency for those who need to trust each other to fall back on surface similarities in an attempt to form a homogeneous group.[8]

Homosocial reproduction constitutes a subtle danger because the perception of similarity usually includes assumptions and expectations about the individual's personality, skills, and likely performance that may not be at all valid.[9] Possible discrepancies may not become apparent immediately. When they do surface, surprise and disillusionment can lead to keen disappointment or other dysfunctional consequences for both the organization and the individual.

It is wise to ask, "Why does the organization want me?" Company representatives may consciously or unconsciously reveal that surface similarities are factors when they say why they think you would fit in. Such remarks as these were made by those who recruited Bob Drake: "We need people like you"; "You are our kind of person"; and "People who look like you do well in our organization." Bob might have taken these as clues to probe further for the underlying meaning of the phrases "like you" and "our kind." What was being alluded to was Bob's athletic, strong physical presence, which apparently led the recruiters to impute to Bob certain values he did not share—extreme aggressiveness and cutthroat competitiveness. If surface characteristics alone are implied in speaking of a good culture fit, you should clarify what the implicit assumptions and expectations are.

Four-Minute Decision

Research indicates that the conventional wisdom about the importance of initial impressions appears to be well founded. Information obtained early has a more significant impact on an interviewer than does information obtained later. This finding has been referred to as the primacy effect. One early study found that, on average, interviewers reached a conclusion about job candidates after only *4 minutes* during a 15-minute interview, or in approximately 25 percent of the time available.[10] This tendency for the real interview to be over shortly after it begins should be noted (and avoided) by both parties.

Interviewer's Agenda

You should keep the personal agenda of the interviewer in mind. It is useful to ask: "Why is this person on my interview schedule? What is the person's stake in this process and his or her personal agenda?"

A recruiter who has a long list of candidates to be interviewed may be looking primarily for reasons to reject candidates. If the recruiter's own performance evaluation by the company is based on a batting average on retention of those hired (the percentage of those the recruiter has recommended who eventually remain with the organization), the recruiter may prefer to play it safe and produce a short list of sure-stayers. On the other hand, if the recruiter's batting average is based on an ability to attract certain kinds of people, such as MBAs or engineers, in a tight hiring market rather than on their record of retention, the recruiter may be more inclined to use enticement or seduction techniques.

Finally, the recruiter may simply be interviewing to add bodies to the denominator of the fraction called the selection ratio, which is the number hired divided by the number interviewed. A low ratio indicates that many people were screened in selecting the chosen few; this is sometimes used to prove the thoroughness of a company's selection procedures. The point is that you should be cognizant of this kind of motivation underlying the interviewer's agenda rather than that measurement systems are prone to this type of misuse.[11]

Recruiting Traps Under Your Control

Self-Seduction

You are tempted to oversell, just as the organization is, and for the same basic reasons.[12] A danger analogous to the organization seducing you is the parallel possibility of self-seduction.

Again, seduction is distinguished from overselling by the critical test of whether you are aware of what is happening. Self-seduction is involved if you lull yourself into making things appear in a favorable light rather than as they really are. Four common patterns or syndromes of self-seduction that I have observed are described in what follows:

1. *Offer-collection syndrome.* Some people attempt to get a great many offers in order to look as good as possible to themselves and others. If asked to explain what they are up to, such a person might say, "I will collect a lot of offers by aggressively selling myself. Having plenty of good options will allow me to pick one that is the best overall fit. In addition, the increased bargaining power will put me in a better position to negotiate my terms." The subtle danger here is failing to recognize that (a) overselling leads to unrealistic expectations on the part of the

organization that are difficult to renegotiate later; (b) the time spent collecting offers could be spent trying to gain a deeper understanding of the organizations one is really interested in, thus permitting a better assessment of culture fit and a smoother entry; and (c) the purpose of collecting offers may be personal ego enhancement rather than having a wider choice or better bargaining power and fit.

2. *Lack of focus.* "I don't know what I want, but if I look around long enough, sooner or later I'll find something I really like." There is nothing wrong with lack of focus if the reasons for it are genuine. Self-seduction is involved, however, if the lack of focus is merely an excuse to avoid the critical thinking and the careful picking and choosing necessary for a more focused search.

3. *Peer pressure.* Perceived pressure from your peers may have to do with what types of industries and organizations are considered desirable and why. You may be responding to the expectations of peers who believe that the higher the starting salaries, the better; or the less time it takes to complete the recruitment process, the better. Such pressures could increase your culture misfit by inducing you to look at industries or companies that would be incompatible with your values, skills, or agenda; to emphasize salary at the cost of other substantive considerations; and to encourage a more superficial job search. Not recognizing these pressures for what they are is another type of self-seduction.

4. *Self-delusion.* When the search gets discouraging, you are more likely to delude yourself into believing that available alternatives are better than they are. During a period of slow offers, you are less likely to keep an open mind and a critical attitude about the available options; you will tend not to probe too deeply for the real meaning of what people in the prospective organization are saying. Another tendency is not to explore certain topics because of not wanting to face up to the information that might come to light.

By playing make-believe, self-seduction promotes inadequate testing in important areas, discourages critical examination of the available information, and leads to suspension of good judgment. These responses may be temporarily soothing, but the brute force of reality will sooner or later have its impact.

The Implicit Favorite

A study of applicants engaged in the recruiting process revealed that they tended to follow this self-seductive sequence[13]:

- At some (unspecified) point in the search process, the individual intuitively selects an implicitly favored job offer.
- A straw man offer is then picked for comparison with the implicit favorite, and the choice is progressively narrowed to these two alternatives.
- Additional information continues to be gathered to make a wise decision, but the game is already over. The individual has selected the implicit favorite and is simply trying to build a case to reject the straw man.

There are two subtle dangers in making choices this way. First, there is the danger of cloaking the decision in a misleading aura of rationality; the rationale is retrospective and justifies a choice made intuitively and perhaps prematurely. Second, although it is natural to look for assurance that you have made the right decision (research confirms that one goes through a period of doubt *after* making a decision), an extended period spent in justifying it is not time well spent.[14]

To deal with this problem, you must acknowledge an implicit favorite as soon as the evidence suggests that it has appeared. You should then explicitly test the implicit favorite against the straw man *and other alternatives* to see if it still holds up. You are likely to make a more carefully reasoned decision, either for or against the implicit favorite, if you investigate objectively with the following attitude: "Since I like the implicit favorite so much, I need to find out exactly why I like it by carefully comparing it to other prospects in terms of its pleasing and special attributes as well as its dangers and not-so-appealing features."

External Justifications

Your decision to join an organization may be made on a rational basis, but if you don't feel real commitment to the decision, you may continue to question the soundness of your choice even after joining the organization. This doubt could hurt your chances for survival and success in the organization.[15]

It is possible to be rational without real commitment because you must feel that you chose the organization and job primarily for their *intrinsic* value in order to feel committed to them. If the organization fits well with your values, skills, and agenda, then the commitment develops. If you explain the choice on the basis of extrinsic factors ("The money was the determining factor," or "I had no other offers"), this external justification hurts real commitment. The danger in not being sensitive to this general tendency is that you may not feel intrinsic commitment simply because external justifications are available.

Manage Your Recruiting

The recruiting traps are treacherous because you may not be conscious of the goals you are setting and the interpretations and evaluations you are making during the recruiting process. As Timothy Wilson explains, the conscious mind is *not* the CEO who delegates work to lower level managers who then do the less important work via unconscious mental processing, because what is typically considered the proper work of consciousness—goal setting, interpretation, evaluation—can also be done unconsciously. Rather, the unconscious and the conscious mind have evolved to serve separate but complementary functions. The unconscious mind is the on-line pattern detector and early warning system concerned with the here and now and generates automatic responses, whereas the conscious mind is the after-the-fact check and balancer, which takes the longer view and generates a slower, intentional, and controllable response.[16]

Wilson explains why people can be out of touch with themselves: "One reason is that people are motivated to have an overly positive view of themselves and avoid looking too closely at their warts and flaws . . . and that, within limits, it is healthy to do so" (2002, p. 91). He also describes the advantage gained by people whose conscious theories are in alignment with their nonconscious personalities: "Surely, however, we do not want our conscious conceptions too out of whack. There are many times when we would be better off recognizing our limitations, abilities, and prospects. When choosing a career, for example, it would be to people's advantage to know whether their nonconscious personalities were better suited for a life as a lawyer, salesperson, or circus performer."[17]

You can guard against the subtle dangers of the recruiting process by taking steps to ensure that your conscious theories and unconscious thinking are in alignment. One way to do this is to ask a number of questions that you may prefer not to think about during the recruiting process. Another way is to use a number of specific techniques that can reveal your unconscious thinking and enable you to consciously consider it to make better decisions.

Here is a list of questions to think about from time to time during the recruiting process:

1. What is my personal agenda? Does it make sense given the agendas of my boss and the other key players?
2. What do I *dislike* most about the organization and job?
3. What am I trying to *avoid* finding out? Is there useful information that I need and can get but am afraid of having to deal with?
4. Am I confusing hopes with expectations?
5. What options do I have if it turns out that I don't like the organization, my job, or my boss? Can I leave the organization or move elsewhere within it? What if my culture misfit is irreconcilable?
6. Am I testing my assumptions and expectations with relevant people inside the organization, with knowledgeable outsiders, and with those who know me well?
7. Am I confusing the question of the organization and the job that will make me look good with the question of where I would be successful and happy?
8. When surprising or ambiguous bits of information crop up, do I rationalize them according to my hopes and desires, or do I further probe them in the spirit of discovery?
9. Do I trust my feelings to guide my inquiry and to complement my analysis, instead of either shutting them out or letting them dominate my thinking?[18]
10. Do I take time to mull over difficult choices, or do I jump to quick conclusions?

One technique for making better decisions is the *balance sheet* procedure developed by Irving Janis and his coworkers.[19] It is designed to facilitate consideration of all relevant positives and negatives from four angles: tangible gains and losses for self, tangible gains and losses for others, self-approval or -disapproval, and approval or disapproval of others.

A second technique, *outcome psychodrama*, is a kind of role-playing exercise conducted under the guidance of a counselor. The counselor asks you to assume that some time has passed since a choice has been made and to speculate aloud on what has happened in that period. You are asked to repeat and expand upon the scenario until all the potential risks and benefits have been flushed out.

A third technique is to keep a recruiting diary to record surprising, confusing, or critical bits and pieces of information from your dealings with a prospective company. Good gauges of when to record something are your intuition and instincts. If something doesn't feel right, it should be recorded rather than discarded. Any one of the recorded items may not mean very much, but together they could reveal a pattern that provides important insights into the organization and yourself.

A fourth technique is to ask a trusted friend[20] to be a sounding board or devil's advocate during the recruiting process, since sympathetic cross-examination can also lead to a more conscious and reasoned process of job choice.

In essence, all these techniques attempt to reveal your unconscious thinking so that you can consciously consider it to make better decisions.

Entry Experiences of Course Alumni

It will not be possible to discern and decode the organization completely prior to accepting a job offer, regardless of how much time and effort you put into it. Students who have taken my course, on which this book is based, were contacted 3 months after they had joined a new organization to find out what they did *not* know at the time they accepted the job.

They said they had misread or missed one or more of the following aspects of the organization.

Organization's Culture

- How the organization pushes people to work harder
- Words the people in the organization use and their true meaning
- Personalities within the culture
- Subcultures in the organization
- Outside versus inside perception of the organization
- Culture at higher levels

Job Challenges

- Specific processes involved to get things done
- Informal channels used
- Pace—faster or slower than anticipated
- Minute-by-minute action

The Key Players and Others

- Who the "jerks" versus the high-status people in the organization are
- How people react to stress and crisis
- Their boss's real agenda

Even though they had not been able to understand their organization fully prior to accepting their job offers, the course alumni said the concepts, frameworks, and tools in this book allowed them to come to terms with the shocks and the surprises they encountered after entry more quickly, and they were able to respond faster and more effectively than they otherwise could have. Their understanding that all cannot be known prior to entry—and also that shocks are common and that it is possible to recover—helped these people to persevere with greater speed and confidence when there were setbacks.

How Much Time and Effort Should
You Put Into Recruiting?

Since all cannot be known prior to entry, it makes little sense to become overly anxious about a new job and organization prior accepting their offer. It is certainly important to avoid an *irreconcilable* misfit with the key players and with the organization's culture. For the rest, a lot depends on your flexibility. Those who are more adaptive can afford to place less emphasis on knowing the organization prior to joining it.

Besides, as the course alumni reported, you cannot know the organization fully no matter how much time and effort you put into it during recruiting. At least two other factors, which you do not control in the short run, are important (Figure 11). One is bargaining power. Those who have more bargaining power are likely to receive more offers and to feel confident in probing deeper to understand the organizations they are considering joining. Marketability can be increased over the long haul by enhancing your knowledge and skills, but it cannot be changed in the short term. Luck can also play a role. For example, you may find few job openings available if you are in the job market when the economy is bad. Even if you have done a good job of understanding your organization prior to entry, you may discover later that things have changed because of circumstances or events that could not have been anticipated—for example, changes in key organizational personnel

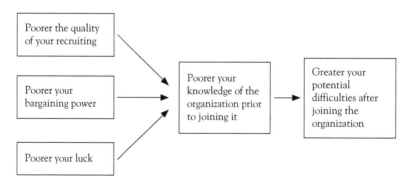

Figure 11 Factors influencing your knowledge of the organization prior to joining

caused by turnover or death that could not possibly have been foreseen by you.

So how much time and effort should you put into recruiting? First, the less the time and effort you put in, the poorer your understanding of the organization and the greater the potential difficulties for you after entry. Second, since factors other than the quality of your recruiting are important, it does not pay to become *obsessive* about your recruiting. *If all you do is to try to anticipate a better tomorrow, there is no time to live well today.* It pays to avoid being either paranoid or cavalier in your recruiting efforts and to keep your antennae, awareness, and flexibility high in preparing to enter a new organization.

Bob Drake erred in the direction of being cavalier. He had five very good job offers, and two of them seemed to be a much better fit for him than the one he accepted. Unfortunately, Bob didn't adequately investigate this. Instead, he conducted a lengthy but superficial job search and succumbed to organizational seduction, homosocial reproduction, self-seduction (offer-collection syndrome, lack of focus, peer pressure), and implicit favorite. Bob did not gain very much as a result, with one important exception: Bob did learn from his traumatic experience and took steps to do a better job of assessing and entering the next organization he joined, where he has done very well. However, he paid dearly for this lesson.

Summary

You need to find out as much as possible about the keys to creating a positive impact for your organization and yourself (Keys #1 to #4, Part I) *prior* to accepting a new job (Key #5), but several difficulties in the recruiting process can derail this effort. Key #6 shows you how to overcome these difficulties by interviewing smartly and probing carefully during the actual recruiting.

One difficulty is that you cannot ask the people you are interviewing about sensitive matters directly. You have to begin with important questions that people are willing to answer before venturing into more sensitive areas. You also have to rely on available documents and your observations of the people you meet, and what you see as well as what you do not see, and draw reasonable inferences from these data.

Other difficulties are the traps that plague the recruiting process. You must recognize and sidestep traps of the organization's making, and avoid the traps that you may set for yourself.

If you are an adaptive and flexible person, you can afford to place less emphasis on knowing all there is to know about a new job and organization prior to accepting their offer because you can adjust and adapt quickly after joining—as long as there is no *irreconcilable* misfit with the key players or with the organization's culture. Regardless, it makes little sense to become overly anxious or paranoid about the recruiting process because your bargaining power and your luck also influence what you can know prior to accepting a new job (Figure 11).

PART III

Talk Less and Listen More for Effective Onboarding

Your chances of knowing what you need to know about a new job and organization prior to accepting their offer (Part I) are increased by following the guidelines presented in Part II. To that extent, your entry into a new job and organization is made less difficult.

Nevertheless, no matter how good your apparent knowledge of a new job and organization prior to accepting their offer, the first few weeks and months after entry will be a period when surprises, trials, and tribulations are bound to occur. That is the subject of Part III.

A number of forces, both subtle and not-so-subtle, lead newcomers—whether just out of college[1] or more seasoned[2]—to sow the seeds of their own downfall. Key #7 shows you how and why this happens, and what you can do about it. Key #8 offers guidance for monitoring your progress in a new job and for whether you should settle in or move on.

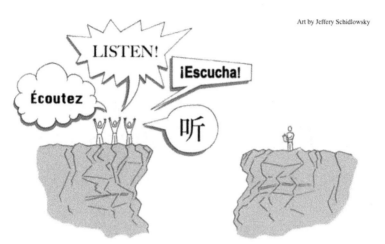

Art by Jeffery Schidlowsky

Talk Less and Listen More for Effective Onboarding

KEY #7

Survive and Contribute as a Newcomer

Research in a wide variety of organizational settings has shown that newcomers are particularly vulnerable—what has been called the "liability of newness"—and also that an individual's early organizational experiences strongly influence his or her later contribution and advancement in the organization.[1] This being the case, the first few weeks and months in a new job deserve to be managed particularly well. Unfortunately, a variety of factors conspire to make this a particularly stressful and difficult period.[2] Key #7 will help you to understand and better manage this crucial early period.

You face special difficulties as a newcomer for three main reasons: (1) You do not know the organization's culture, your job challenges, and the expectations and agendas of your key players and others as well as you will come to know them later on; (2) You have not yet shown that you can do your job well and make other contributions to your organization; and (3) You have not yet built good relationships with your key players and others, and therefore you have little or no credibility in their eyes.[3]

This is why the survival rate of new managers is low, as the results of a survey by Right Management Consultants confirm—these statistics are based on a wealth of data that the firm's coaches have collected from their clients over the years.[4]

1. Thirty-five percent of managers who change jobs fail in their new ones and either quit or are asked to leave within 18 months.
2. Failure to build strong relationships with peers and subordinates is the chief culprit in 61 percent of new hires and promotions that don't work out.

What can you do to improve your odds? First, you can continue to learn about the organization after entry. The questions to think about that you could not answer prior to entry (Key #5) must be reviewed periodically and answers must be sought. Second, you can apply Keys #1 to #4 in Part I to start creating a positive impact for your organization and yourself.

Continue to Learn About the Organization After Entry

As a newcomer you feel overwhelmed by unfamiliar faces, names, titles, work roles, and locations. Questions come up about how to use your time, where to go, what to do, what to wear, and how to behave, as well as questions about your relationships, friendships, competence, and expectations about the work to be done. The better your understanding of the organization prior to entry, the smaller this handicap, but there will be a lot to learn about the organization after entry in any case.

The learning curve for newcomers is steep for the first 6 to 10 months. Not all learning takes place at the same time.[5] Technical jargon and special terminology used in the organization are typically tackled first. Without it, you cannot understand enough of what is being communicated to determine what information is important.[6] Next comes an understanding of the essential aspects of the industry, business, company, and job. Knowledge of the culture as well as the social and political realities usually comes last because these matters are more sensitive.

The organization Bob Drake joined was very secretive. Bob's boss was reclusive, and peers gave Bob little or no help. As his frustration with the organization mounted, Bob began to voice some of his concerns to the few people in the organization he felt were being open with him. He later learned that one of these "friends" had communicated Bob's frustrations to others in the organization, including Bob's boss's boss. Had he understood his organization, Bob might have talked less and listened more in order to contribute and survive.

It takes time, perhaps several months, to know who you can trust, who the phonies might be, the personalities and quirks of the key players, the subtleties of the business, the nuances of the industry, and other idiosyncrasies germane to the situation. Unfortunately, an understanding of these realities is also critical to early success.[7]

It pays to formulate some understanding of these realities as quickly as possible and to reassess them periodically. The necessary learning can take place more rapidly if you: (1) learn from available information, (2) proactively develop your information sources and networks, and (3) anticipate and manage culture shocks.

Continue to Learn From Available Information

Everyday conversations and observations provide raw material that can be used to learn about the organization. The rate at which this learning occurs depends on your capacity for absorbing routine information and making sense of it. Insightful learning requires that you avoid the temptation to jump to quick conclusions. You should test interpretations of daily events and occurrences with established members of the organization or knowledgeable others. If discrepancies show up, these must be explored further to understand their underlying significance.

Under what conditions will insiders[8] share their knowledge about these matters with you? The first condition is an organization culture that encourages such disclosure. A second is your demonstration of the ability to use sensitive information with discretion. A third is your possession of something else to offer in trade. Thus, the speed with which you can proactively develop valid information sources depends not only on what the culture prescribes but also on your resourcefulness.

Some companies assign a coach to see that newcomers are properly instructed, advised, groomed, and guided into the organization. A good coach can make an enormous difference in the quality of your entry experience and can help you to learn the organization quickly.[9] If your company does not assign a coach, try to recruit one informally.

Continue to Learn by Proactively Developing Information Sources and Networks

It helps to develop contacts outside your organizational unit and also outside the organization at large—for example, with suppliers, customers, and other industry players. These sources can offer information and a perspective about your situation that you cannot get from insiders.

Don't isolate yourself; take the initiative to reach out to others and learn from them.[10]

Continue to Learn by Anticipating and Managing Culture Shocks

From time to time you may also experience a *culture shock*.[11] An example is the rude awakening or painful revelation that occurs when you discover a major discrepancy between your expectations and hopes, and what the organization is really like.[12] The greater your culture misfit, and the poorer your understanding of your misfit prior to entry, the more intense the shocks will be. These shocks signal that you have not yet understood the organization, and they are best viewed as traumatic but opportune invitations to learn the organizational realities.

It is important to realize that your perspective as a newcomer is conditioned by the culture of the school or other organization you *just came from*. For example, different business schools forge different student cultures, which have important implications for the graduates.[13] It helps to approach early encounters with others in the new organization with an inquisitive rather than a judgmental attitude, while looking and listening for the underlying *meanings* of what people say and do.

Bob Drake, for example, reacted to the shocks he experienced upon entry with disappointment and anger. Had Bob viewed these as clues to *understanding* the organization, he might have learned their underlying significance. The cultural values of the business school Bob had graduated from, and of the organization he had worked for prior to that, were ordered very differently from those of his new company. Where he had studied and worked previously, cooperation prevailed over internal competition; in his new company, it was the other way around. Had he grasped this in the beginning, he might have been able to take appropriate action.

Apply Keys #1 to #4 in Part I to Start Creating a Positive Impact for Your Organization and Yourself

You must begin with the right attitude. Professor Edgar Schein concluded from his study of a panel of MIT alumni as follows:

I got the impression that those few graduates who accepted the human organization, with all its foibles, as a reality soon learned to apply their analytical abilities and high intelligence to getting their jobs done within it, but that those who resisted this reality at an emotional level used up their energy in denial and complaint rather than in problem solving. The "selling," and " compromising," and "politicking" necessary to get their ideas accepted were seen as "selling out" to some lower[-]value system. The same person who would view a complex technical problem as a great challenge found the human problem illegitimate and unworthy of his efforts. The unlearning of this attitude may be one of the key processes in becoming an effective supervisor and manager. At the time I interviewed the alumni, most of them were still in a state of shock and had not begun to reexamine or unlearn this attitude, however.[14]

These findings are not peculiar to the particular sample Professor Schein studied. Other graduates are susceptible to the same danger.[15]

Your key players and others will have a wait-and-see attitude until you prove yourself worthy in the new situation. Some in the organization will want to see you succeed and will offer help, but they may also have unrealistic expectations of you. Others may feel threatened by you and consciously or subconsciously try to precipitate your failure. If you commit too many errors early on, it might be impossible to recover lost ground. Given these difficulties, your feelings at entry are somewhat akin to the stage fright experienced by new actors and actresses—apprehension about performing up to their own and others' expectations in the glare of organizational publicity.[16]

You can apply the four keys in Part I to create a positive impact for your organization and yourself even though you don't know the culture, your job challenges, or your key players and others as well as you will later on. You can (1) conform to the cultural norms until you have performed your job well, made other contributions, and built your credibility; (2) recognize and deal with the job challenges of your first assignments; and (3) begin to develop good relationships with your key players and others by understanding their agendas, and by managing the critical incidents that you might encounter in dealing with them.

Apply Key #1: Conform to the Cultural Norms (Culture Map, Figure 5, Page 19)

The duration of your "honeymoon" with the new organization will vary depending on your particular circumstances, but it will rarely exceed 90 days. You might be able to take necessary action that violates the cultural norms during this period, but after that it will be costly and difficult to do so. Others may openly refuse to cooperate. More often and much more frustratingly, associates may agree to help and appear to be cooperative but you find that nothing substantive gets done.

Where appropriate action does not require the cooperation of others, you may be able to violate the cultural norms if you can bear the associated personal risks. As a general rule, however, it is best to conform to the culture until you have demonstrated that you can do your job well, made other valued contributions, developed good relationships with your key players and others, and built your credibility with them.

Apply Key #2: Understand Your Job Challenges in Your First Assignments

The *first* assignments have great symbolic and substantive significance. Getting off to a good start contributes immeasurably to creating a favorable first impression. Also, doing a job well often leads to liking the job more, and both tend to enhance self-esteem.[17] Higher self-esteem increases the likelihood of success on subsequent assignments; and as the cycle repeats itself, a success syndrome develops.[18]

It seldom pays to plunge in to do the first assignments *as they are stated*. It is more sensible to find out what the real assignment is, what is really valued, and especially to know if it is a phony or impossible assignment.

Is the Stated Assignment Your Real Assignment?

Any discrepancy between the stated and the real assignment can be discovered by thinking about questions such as these and trying to get the answers:

What is the agenda of the key players?

- Are bait-and-switch, bait-and-keep, or bait-and-eat techniques at work? (Question 18, Key #5)
- What criteria will the key players and others use to evaluate my performance and contributions?

Your key players will look at not just the achievement of valued results but also at *how* the results were achieved. They will be thinking about whether you conducted yourself and got the job done in a manner that increased their confidence in you.

Can You Give Me a Little History?

Much can be learned about the real assignment by thinking about and appropriately asking for some background information with questions such as the following:

- Who was the last person to work on this assignment (or a similar assignment)?
- What happened in that case? Why?
- What has experience taught us about the obstacles and roadblocks that might be encountered in such assignments, and how might they be overcome?
- Who are likely to be opposed to this assignment? Who are likely to support it? Why?

Subsequent probing, if it is done judiciously, can uncover potentially valuable background information. The main thing to recognize is that most assignments have a technical, political, social, and cultural history that you ignore at your peril. It is foolish to proceed without attempting to learn the lessons of this history.

Is Your First Assignment Phony?

If you begin as a trainee you may find your first assignment to be a meaningless practice session or a Mickey Mouse exercise. Newcomers who begin their jobs by going through a formal in-house training program may have similar reactions. Many companies recognize that this kind of introduction to a new job can demotivate newcomers, particularly those with high potential, and they try to avoid lengthy full-time training programs or unchallenging early assignments.[19] In organizations that use a demoralizing initiation, what can you do to manage the situation better?

First, you must recognize that your boss and higher-ups may not trust you with large doses of responsibility until you have proven yourself. As you prove yourself, more challenging and responsible work will be given to you. Second, the level of challenge in the first assignment does not necessarily reflect their level of confidence in you. It may just happen that there is not enough challenging work to assign to you when you arrive. Or assignments may have been created for you to fill time while you wait for the real job they have in mind for you.

Finally, having understood why an initial assignment may be phony, you can view this slack period as an opportunity to *create* meaningful assignments and make valued contributions. If it is done with sensitivity, this can help the organization and demonstrate your ability to take initiative. You can also use this time to learn about the organization.

Is Your First Assignment a Mission Impossible?

You might be confronted with a first assignment that carries *too much* responsibility and challenge. Such an impossible mission may mean that those who commissioned you to the task grossly overestimated your skills or organizational knowledge. Or the person giving the assignment, typically the boss, may feel threatened by you and is consciously or unconsciously trying to make you fail. This failure can then be treated as evidence that "the new kid on the block is not that great after all." Sometimes an impossible task is assigned to chasten the newcomer; Professor Schein provides a classic example:

> An engineering manager . . . gave every new college graduate who entered his group the task of analyzing a special circuit[,] which violated some textbook assumptions and therefore looked as though it could not work, yet which had been sold for years. When the new employee would announce that the circuit could not work, he was told that it did and was asked to figure out why.

He typically could not explain it, which left him thoroughly de-
pressed and chastened about the value of his college education.
The manager felt that only at this point was the new employee
"ready" to learn something and to tackle some of the "real" problems on which the company was working.[20]

Such "upending experiences," as Schein calls them, are designed to
"unfreeze" the newcomer by dramatically violating his or her basic assumptions about self or organization and to predispose him or her to
learn the required new values, skills, and agendas.

It is easier to develop a strategy for dealing with impossible assignments if you recognize them for what they are. Communicating more
valid information about yourself may reduce unrealistic assessments and
expectations that others have of you. This is usually in your self-interest
in the longer term because it increases the chances of starting out well and
letting the success syndrome take hold.

If the people responsible for the assignment are feeling threatened by
you, the situation is trickier. Renegotiating the assignment, refusing it, or
transferring to a different work unit and boss in the same company are
three alternatives, but each faces obvious difficulties.

For example, one new manager in a nonprofit organization thought
her boss was expecting too much of her too soon in order to "break her,"
rather than to break her in. She believed that both her talent and his
sexist attitude were causing him to feel threatened by her. After attempting to work with and around him for a while, she decided to transfer
to a different unit in the same organization. She flourished in the new
unit, delivered high performance, made other valuable contributions, and
eventually rose far above her first boss, who might well have blocked her
had she remained in his unit.

Apply Keys #3 and #4: Develop Good Relationships and Gain Credibility With Your Key Players and Others

It takes 12 to 18 months to develop a good relationship. The process by
which this occurs is described in what follows, based on the work of John
Gabarro.[21]

The process occurs in four basic stages: learning, exploration, testing, and stabilization.

A Good Relationship Evolves Over Four Stages

The four stages of the process do not have distinct beginnings and endings, but they do occur in sequence. The duration of each phase is unpredictable; the critical thing to remember is that, although there is a great deal of variation, it usually takes between 12 and 18 months to develop a good relationship. If you feel that you have developed a good relationship in 3 or 4 months, for example, try to determine what stage the relationship is really in.

In building relationships, both parties work out an interpersonal contract—a tacit but agreed-upon set of expectations concerning roles and performance, trust and influence. The effectiveness of a relationship depends on *how* the two parties progress through the stages of the process. Good relationships evolve when both parties clarify their expectations early on, explore their specific expectations in detail, surface and negotiate their differences, and test and work through the bases and limits of trust and influence before the relationship stabilizes. If the relationship and the contract reach a stabilization point too early, the exploration and testing have been too superficial, and the relationship subsequently becomes destabilized while the interpersonal contract unravels.

Much of the learning, exploration, testing, and negotiation involved in developing good relationships takes place during routine interactions in the course of a typical workday. Critical incidents (such as the discovery that one party has intentionally withheld important information) serve either to crystalize or dramatically alter the accumulated experience. A good relationship cannot be built if the interactions and the critical incidents are poorly managed.[22]

Manage Your Interactions With Others

The first encounters are important. It is best to show respect and give others the benefit of the doubt when strange or senseless behavior is observed. Try to make sense of it by asking yourself the following questions:

- *Why* do these seemingly reasonable people do these seemingly unreasonable things?
- What is it that *I* don't understand that will allow me to see that this apparently senseless behavior is perfectly sensible?

You may discover that some people are in fact unreasonable and that others behave in a senseless manner, but these are conclusions you should reach based on evidence from multiple sources over time rather than judgments you make on first impressions. In your first interactions with others, it is best to listen more and talk less.

It is difficult to know with whom it is safe to be open when you are new. It may take from several months to more than a year to accumulate sufficient evidence to know if there are any phonies or spies in the organization who cannot be trusted. Meanwhile, it is best to listen and observe more and confide less. Your trust with others will build as the number of your positive encounters with them increases.

There is a natural tendency for newcomers to feel some anxiety in dealing with authority figures and other powerful people. Try to overcome these feelings and move *toward* power figures ("the electricity") as the opportunity presents itself. ("Don't avoid electricity, but don't get electrocuted!") For example, it is important to try and develop a good relationship not only with your boss, but with his or her boss as well (see I(c) in Exhibit 1, page 4). That way you have a chance to better understand the perspectives and the pressures your boss has to deal with. If there is clear evidence that your boss feels threatened by you, informal access to his or her boss can give you the opportunity to address this issue without escalating it.

If you find yourself moving *away* from the power figures (via reduced contact or increased physical distance), it is a warning sign that you may be a culture misfit—because the values of the powerful people are likely to reflect the organization's culture. Also, if you do not feel comfortable with the powerful people, you are not likely to advance in the organization either.

Bob Drake, for example, had diminishing contact with his boss and the other key players, and his office was moved farther from his boss's office after 3 months on the job. Bob felt relieved, but did not recognize that his sense of relief was in fact a warning signal of his misfit with the organization's culture, and his falling credibility with his boss and the other key players.

Manage Your Critical Incidents

From time to time you will experience a *critical incident*. Examples are an interaction with your key players or others that could become a turning point in your relationship with them, or a discovery that someone has intentionally withheld important information. Such critical incidents may crystalize or dramatically alter your relationships with these people.

To better manage these critical incidents, it pays to compare the agendas of your key players and others who are important to your survival and success (Exhibit 1, page 4) with your own agenda periodically. This review will help you to create a frame of mind that allows you to better respond to various situations as they arise. Critical incidents usually occur spontaneously, with little time for thought or reflection. Being sensitive to your own and others' agendas increases the likelihood that your reflexes and reactions will be appropriate.

After a critical incident, ask yourself: "Did the quality of my relationship with this person improve or diminish as a result of how I managed this interaction or critical incident? Did I gain or lose credibility with this person?" Keep a log of your postentry experiences; the pattern that emerges is an indication of the quality of your emerging relationships with your key players and others.

Your *Advantages* as a Newcomer

The difficulties of being a newcomer should not blind you to its advantages. These can be utilized to the benefit of both the organization and yourself.[23]

One advantage you have is the *honeymoon* period. You should use this period to learn about the organization, by violating the cultural norms if necessary. This may be tolerated during your honeymoon because others think you don't know any better. However, deviant behavior can backfire if you appear not to have learned the culture long after the period it normally takes to do so.

Another advantage you have is *low equity*. Since your stake in the organization is low relative to that of an established member, you can take more personal risk to help the organization and yourself. If things don't work out, you can leave with a smaller loss of investment of your time and effort.[24] For example, MBA Mark Wyman began his managerial career as the foreman of a work group that was performing well below what Mark thought the group could put out if certain changes in work methods were made. Mark's boss wasn't enthusiastic; other supervisors told him that higher-ups didn't like needless experimentation and wouldn't tolerate mistakes. Mark had prior production experience and decided to proceed with the changes after getting his boss's acquiescence. ("Go ahead, but don't screw up!") Mark was confident of his approach and believed that the immediate improvements in results that he expected would speak for themselves. He also believed he had less to lose than his reticent peers who had been with the company much longer and appeared unwilling to rock the boat. Mark's subsequent success benefited both the organization and himself.

A third asset you have is *objectivity*. Since you don't have an organizational ax to grind and are not vested in past decisions, you could be valuable as an unbiased source of information and opinion. You are also more likely to be *perceived as unbiased* owing to your newness, so you are in a better position to understand different points of view in the organization. You can put this advantage to good use by not taking sides early on. Objectivity permits you to take dispassionate action as well.

Fourth, you have an opportunity to bring a *fresh perspective* to the organization. You can help the people in the organization better understand themselves and their culture, and can provide the organization with new ideas and insights. Finally, you bring *new skills and values* that could benefit both the organization and yourself.

Unfortunately, as in the case of Bob Drake, both newcomers and established members often conduct their affairs in a manner that make these contributions difficult. But by learning about the organization and applying Keys #1 to #4 in Part I, you can survive and create a positive impact for both the organization and yourself as a newcomer.

Summary

Key #7 shows you how to avoid the fate of the 35 percent who fail in their new jobs within the first 18 months. You must learn as much as you can, as fast as you can—about the culture, the job challenges, and the key players—using available information, by proactively developing your information sources and networks, and by anticipating and managing culture shocks.

To perform your job well and contribute quickly as a newcomer, it may be best to initially conform to the cultural norms (Figure 5, Key #1, page 19), understand what the real assignment is, try to avoid phony or impossible first assignments, and take the necessary steps to ensure that you are not among the 61 percent of new hires who fail to develop strong relationships with others in their first 18 months on the job.

Fortunately, it is not all about overcoming difficulties. You have several advantages as a newcomer—honeymoon period, low equity, perceived objectivity, a fresh perspective, and new skills—which you can put to good use to do your job well and make other valued contributions even as a newcomer, and help yourself in the process too.

We turn next to the important initial assessments and adjustments you must make in order to determine whether to settle into the organization and get established, or to move on.

KEY #8

Monitor Your Progress to Settle In or Move On

Key #8 shows you how to monitor your progress during the first few weeks and months after joining a new organization to determine if it is a place where you can survive and be successful (Figure 1, page 3).

To make this determination, you must find out how your performance and other contributions are being perceived by your key players and others. If you are doing well, what can you do better? If things are not going well, what are your options? You can apply the four keys to creating a positive impact for your organization and yourself (Part I) to diagnose your situation and take appropriate action.

If the situation is hopeful and you want to continue in the organization, you must signal your intention to remain. If your situation is hopeless, it may be best to leave if you can find another job and organization where you can survive and be successful.

How Do Your Key Players Perceive Your Performance and Other Contributions?

There are two basic ways to find out: by asking for feedback and by reading the tea leaves.

Ask for Feedback

You need the perspective of your key players and others to know how you are doing. Your performance appraisal, typically within the first year, can provide helpful feedback but this may not be soon enough to be of help. You can increase the chances of getting timely feedback by letting your key players and others know *early on* that you would like feedback *prior to* the 6-month or annual review.[1] If you have a short first assignment— for example, in a consulting firm—you can request such feedback at the end of this task if it is not automatically given. If you have a longer first assignment, you might request feedback at the end of the first month or the first 3 months.

There is a danger of appearing overly anxious or lacking in confidence by asking for such early feedback, but a lot depends on how the request is made. If you indicate that you find early feedback helpful, and don't make a big deal in asking for it, you will probably get it without any problem. For example, you might say, "I don't know about others, but I find such feedback to be extremely useful to quickly get up to speed. Is it possible to get such feedback here?" If you get honest feedback early on, the resulting insight into what is really valued in the organization, and how your job performance and other contributions are perceived by your key players and others, will be of great help to you.

The appropriateness of the request for early feedback also depends on your position in the organization. If you are in an entry-level position, you may be able to make such a request more easily. In a higher position, you may find it more difficult because others may expect you to be more self-assured and able to make such judgments on your own.

You must avoid organizational phonies and be careful about whom to trust, but it is generally unwise to draw conclusions about how you are doing silently. You can talk to your coach (if you have one), fellow new-comers, peers, your key players, and others as appropriate to get multiple perspectives on how they see your job performance and other contributions. Without the benefit of others' impressions and judgments, including those from outside your department/division, you don't really know how your job performance and other contributions are being perceived.

Read the Tea Leaves

Your salary *increase* after joining the organization is an important indicator of how your key players and others perceive your job performance and other contributions—not the absolute amount or the percentage increase so much as the percentage increase relative to others in a similar bracket.

Your boss, coach, or peers may be able to provide the organizational perspective needed to help you to understand what each raise means.[2]

Another important indication of how your job performance and other contributions are perceived is what kind of *second* assignment (and subsequent ones) you are given. The first assignment, whether phony or challenging, was made with limited information and some preconceived notions about you. The second and later assignments, however, are made with the knowledge of what you have actually accomplished in the organization. The change in degree of responsibility from the first to the second and subsequent assignments is the significant index. As in deciphering the implication of salary increases, however, you should have a clear perspective on the situation and hear what your key players and others have to say before drawing any conclusions. For example, they may have valued your initial contribution but there may have been no important assignments available to give you.

Other indications of how your job performance and other contributions are seen are the company perks and symbolic gestures. Examples are assignment of a private office, use of a company car, stock options, and appointment to prestigious committees in the organization.[3]

Apply Keys #1 to #4 in Part I to Diagnose Your Situation and Take Appropriate Action

Apply Key #1: Are You a Good Fit? Is There a Misfit? Is It Irreconcilable?

As you accumulate experience in the new job, you get a better feel for your fit with the key players and with the organization's culture, and the resulting impact for you and your organization. However, such recognition builds slowly and may be hard to accept. The tendency to ignore or repress the growing evidence of a poor fit may go on for too long until a critical incident or a culture shock finally crystalizes it for you. Bob Drake, for example, didn't really grasp the extent of his misfit with his boss and the organization's culture until his first performance appraisal 6 months after joining, when he was fired.

You should periodically review the assessment you made prior to entry to see if a reappraisal of your fit with the key players or with the organization's culture is warranted in light of your deepening understanding of the situation. You may encounter two common dilemmas. One is that the fit looks better for the longer term than for the short term. For example, an MBA brought into a volunteer organization as part of an effort to bring a more analytical orientation to the organization remained a culture misfit until the culture of this volunteer organization eventually changed to place greater emphasis on analysis.

A related situation is that your fit looks bleak in your department/division but looks brighter elsewhere in the larger organization. In that case you may have to consider (1) withdrawing immediately from the department/division and relocating elsewhere in the organization; (2) withdrawing from the department/division later on, after building bridges to other parts of the organization; or (3) remaining and either waiting out the problem or attempting to influence changes in the department/division to make it a more attractive place to continue working.

If there is an irreconcilable misfit, it may be best for you to leave if you can. Biting the bullet may be less costly for both you and the organization than an eventual withdrawal or dismissal.

In general, because some degree of misfit is commonplace, neither you nor the organization is likely to gain very much unless you are willing to reexamine at least some of your personal beliefs and values.[4] The key players or the culture of the next organization you join may not be a better fit for you. The inherent difficulties that created such misfits in the first place remain. If you are looking for a "perfect fit" you may change jobs or enterprises more than once, only to discover similar or different misfits with the other organizations. Repeated failures to attain your ideal fit can cause you to feel acute disappointment, disillusionment, a loss of idealism, and even progressive cynicism.[5]

To avoid such a fate, you might ponder questions such as these: Am I resisting the organization's beliefs and values because they are fundamentally incompatible with my own? Or is it because they imply new behaviors and skills that I am afraid I will not be able to learn? If you adopt the "alter your behavior first" strategy, changes in your corresponding beliefs and values may follow.[6]

The key is to be flexible without compromising important aspects of self. Initially at least, you are only required to comply with the cultural norms;

that is, to *behave* as prescribed by the culture (Figure 5, page 19). Internalization of the corresponding beliefs and values (buying into them) may come later after you have had time to develop better personal relationships[7] in the organization. Such flexibility and creative individualism is ultimately in the best interest of both you and the organization.[8]

Apply Key #2: Are Your Skills, Your Effort, and the Support You Receive to Do Your Job Sufficient in Light of Your Job Challenges?

If not, is it because you do not have the right skills, are not putting in the necessary effort, or are not receiving the required support? Which specific challenges seem to be too great for you? If it is the technical or business challenges, can they be overcome relatively quickly via education and training? If learning from the school-of-hard-knocks is critical, how long will this take? Sometimes the people/political challenges are the toughest. The personalities may be so difficult or the politics so intractable that these challenges may seem to be insurmountable, but there are ways to deal with these challenges (see Key #9, under "Emotional Conflict").

If you conclude that you cannot adequately address your job challenges despite your best efforts, you should talk to your boss, and his or her boss if necessary, to see if you can be moved to a different job—either in the same department/division or elsewhere within the larger organization—that is a much better fit for you. Too many people are too proud to ask for such a re-positioning, fearing that it may reflect poorly on them, and stay on in their jobs only to fail. It is in the best interest of both you and the organization for you to be placed in a position in which you can succeed.

Apply Keys #3 and #4: Are You Building Good Relationships and Gaining Credibility With Your Key Players and Others?

The quality of your relationships and the extent of your credibility with your key players and others can be gauged in several ways:

- Initiation rites that indicate your acceptance by them. Examples are celebrations and events in which your contributions are recognized by them. These rituals and symbols reflect the emotional tone of your relationships with them.

- Their sharing with you of organizational secrets, such as unreported, private, and possibly embarrassing aspects of the organization and its people:
  - Specific technologies, marketing techniques, or production methods, which must not be revealed to competitors.
  - Informal procedures that have to be followed for internal political reasons, and the key people to watch out for.
  - What really happened around key historical events, such as the real reason why a certain product or program was discontinued, or what really happened to the key person who took early retirement.

Your key players and others are making themselves vulnerable to you by revealing these secrets, since you can use the information to embarrass them or hurt the organization. Sharing such information is an especially important indication that they trust you.

Once you have gauged the quality of your relationships with your key players and others, you can work on improving these relationships:

- Assess which stage each relationship is in. (Key #7: learning, exploration, testing, or stabilization?)
- Assess the extent to which you have the three critical ingredients of good relationships. (Key #3: Are you clear about their expectations of you? Is there an agenda mismatch? Do they trust you? Do you have the power to influence them?)

Make a Decision to Stay or Leave

If your review of the keys to creating a positive impact for your organization and yourself indicates that you will not be successful (Figure 1, page 3) and you decide to leave, the process of leave-taking deserves some attention.[9] How you depart from an organization affects your reputation, and the quality of that reputation is based partly on your impact on the people left behind.

If you decide to stay, you must *signal* this intention appropriately to your boss and other key players. Edgar Schein has provided a good discussion of how to do this, as summarized in the following section.[10]

Signal Your Intention to Remain

In many organizations, the intention to remain or leave is not discussed openly. A person who decides to leave customarily finesses the situation by keeping his or her intentions secret until just prior to departure. If you are in such an organization, you must find some indirect means of communicating your intention to remain. Of course, if your organization encourages open dialogue on this question, you can make your intention known directly.

One way of communicating your intention to remain is by demonstrating your commitment to the organization with high energy, long working hours, willingness to do extras, and enthusiasm for your work. Since these are some of the indicators that many organizations use to gauge an employee's intention to remain, you may be misunderstood if you *fail* to signal your intentions in a culturally appropriate way, even though you are performing well, making other valued contributions, are happy with the organization, and want to remain.

You can also communicate your intention to remain by tolerating various kinds of constraints, delays, or undesirable work as temporary conditions. If the organization has promised challenging work, salary increases, and promotions on a schedule that it is not delivering, this could be interpreted as meaning that the organization is rejecting you. However, if you have reason to believe that this is not the case, a willingness to accommodate the inconvenience and put up with the apparent abrogation of the implicit contract is a good symbolic way of communicating your commitment to the organization. However, this behavior can lead to misunderstanding and game playing unless both sides are careful to read each other's actual situation and intentions correctly.

If you intend to remain with the organization and communicate this effectively, and if the organization reciprocates, you can settle in and continue to create a positive impact for your organization and yourself.

Summary

Key #8 advises that, rather than wait for the formal 6-month or annual performance appraisal, you should find out sooner how your key players and others perceive your performance and other contributions in your new job—by requesting early feedback, and by interpreting the significance of a salary increase or a second assignment if you received either of these during this period.

If you find that you are not able to create a positive impact for your organization and for yourself, a review of the four keys in Part I should help you to understand why. Is it because your misfit with the key players in the organization or its culture is too great or irreconcilable? Is it because you do not have the skills, are not able to put in the effort, and/or do not receive sufficient support to do your job? Is it because you are not able to build good relationships with your key players or others?

If your situation looks bleak, it may be best to move on if you have better options. If the situation looks bright, you can settle in, and continue to improve your job performance and make other contributions to the organization in ways that also create positive outcomes for you. The multiple ways in which you can do this are covered in Part IV.

PART IV

Continue to Deliver Results and Make Other Contributions

This part of the book examines how you can continue to deliver results and make other contributions in order to create a positive impact for your organization and yourself as your career progresses.

Key #9 describes how to leverage the organization's culture—and how to navigate it even if you are a culture misfit—in order to do your job well and make other valued contributions to your organization. How to manage conflict in order to do what is right is also considered. Although some of these actions may run the risk of disrupting one or more of your relationships in the organization, and might even diminish your credibility with some people in the short run, you can help the organization and yourself in the long run by taking action that may be unconventional or unpopular but important and necessary.

Key #10 shows how you can also contribute by becoming a manager, a leader, and an entrepreneur. There is controversy in the literature about whether one person can become all three—or even two of the three[1]—and there is confusion as well about what these labels mean. Fortunately, both confusion and controversy disappear when managers, leaders, and entrepreneurs are defined in terms of their *contributions*—that is, the *results* they deliver—rather than in terms of their personality traits or behaviors.

Managers improve efficiency; they help the organization to do more with less. Leaders create a vision of the future and the necessary change to achieve it. Entrepreneurs seize new business opportunities. One may disagree with the label (manager, leader, entrepreneur) used in connection with a particular contribution. For example, some may argue that a manager's contribution includes what we have defined as the contribution of a leader. But no one can doubt that *all* of these contributions are valuable.

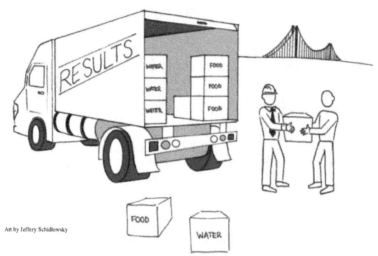

Art by Jeffery Schidlowsky

Continue to Deliver Results and Make Other Contributions

KEY #9

Contribute by Leveraging Your Organization's Culture and Managing Conflict

Key #9 first shows you how you can leverage the organization's culture to do your job well and make other valued contributions, even if you are a culture misfit. This is followed by a discussion of how to manage conflict in order to do what is right.[1]

Leverage Your Organization's Culture

Your job performance and other contributions can improve if you (1) remain attuned to the organization's culture and your fit with it, (2) operate in a manner that is culturally acceptable, and (3) acquire the necessary cultural skills.

Remain Attuned to the Organization's Culture and Your Fit With It

As you get established in the organization, you begin to take culture more and more for granted. This is economical because it conserves your limited energy and attention, but it also means that you may be blindsided by the culture. One reason for this is that you may assume that the same culture is present at a higher level in the organization, or in a different part of the organization, when it may not be. Another is that you may assume that the culture is what it was earlier, when in fact it has changed. An important way to remain attuned to the culture, and to your evolving fit with it, is to view the resistance you encounter in organizational life as an *invitation* to better understand yourself and the organization.

Resistance from others may be due to aspects of self that you do not see very well. For example, Jerry Rowland felt that his boss, Rob Zorn, exhibited a passive attitude whenever Jerry came to Rob for advice. Jerry surmised that Rob felt threatened by him and was therefore passively resisting him. He didn't realize that Rob felt irritated by Jerry's repeated requests for advice because Jerry had sold himself as a self-starter who needed little guidance. The problem was that Jerry in fact needed much more direction than he admitted to himself and told others. He might have gained this insight had he reflected more deeply on what lay behind the pattern of resistance he had encountered, not only from his present boss but also from prior bosses. All the evidence clearly indicated that Jerry was not the self-starter that he told himself and others he was. But Jerry could not see it.

Resistance from others in the organization may also indicate that you do not understand the organization as well as you might think. Bob Drake would have better understood his organization's culture, and his fit with it, had he queried in this way. He might have then discovered and addressed his irreconcilable misfit with the culture much sooner than he did.

Operate in a Manner That Is Culturally Acceptable

To leverage the organization's culture, you must operate in a manner that is culturally acceptable. Al Hirsch, the creative and individualistic manager who loved to show off his flashy European cars, was not willing to conform to the egalitarian culture of his organization by coming to work in a more modestly priced car like everyone else did. Roderick Smallwood, the contrasting case, had no problem in conforming on such matters, for it gave him the elbow room he needed to violate the cultural norms when he felt this was necessary to deliver better results.

Acquire the Necessary Cultural Skills

To leverage culture, you also need to acquire the necessary skills. Skill development comes with practice; two areas are particularly important.

Use Words and Symbols with Cultural Sensitivity

Words and symbols can be subtle but powerful tools to activate cultural values in service of the actions you are taking because research has confirmed that they can arouse people's *emotions*.[2] Poor choice of words and symbols can create needless resistance. For example, at Global Bank, Jack Rey labeled the back office a "factory" to draw attention to the production management discipline that needed to be applied to the back office to cope with the rising tide of paper. Although the *concept* made a great deal of sense in light of the challenge, its implementation ran into difficulties for a number of reasons, including resistance from the middle managers. Although the word "factory" clearly and powerfully communicated the intended change, it insulted the back office managers who saw themselves as bankers.

Use of a different word or phrase that respected their self-image while communicating the new concept would have created less resentment. One such phrase that was eventually adopted for the new back office at Global Bank was "services management group." It honored their past (excellent *service* was provided by the old back office) while signaling the need for a new order (the old back office was not *managed* well).

In contrast, at Atlantic Engineering, President James Hightower's astute use of the phrase "phantom plant" drew the attention of his operating people to an inventory problem that they were not addressing. His appointment of the corporate controller as the "plant manager" of the phantom plant was a subtle but effective way of empowering this staff executive. It helped to legitimize the controller's involvement in an operating problem, which the line managers might have otherwise resisted.[3]

The way to develop your language sensitivity is to forget about what the words and symbols mean to *you* and try instead to discern their underlying meanings for the intended audience—and the *emotions* the words evoke for them.[4]

Although sensitive use of words and symbols is extremely important, it will make no difference—and may make things worse by breeding cynicism—if your deeds do not match your message, or if you lack genuine empathy for the people you are trying to reach. Spin doctors, beware!

Develop Argumentation Skills[5]

Closely related to the sensitive use of words and symbols is the skill in arguing for the proposed course of action in ways that honor rather than discredit the organization's cultural values. Those who are skillful in arguing that their position is in keeping with the highest cultural values are likely to gain advantage. Similarly, all other things being equal, those who can authentically represent themselves as the cultural guardians will have an upper hand.

Perform and Contribute Even If You Are a Culture Misfit

There are four basic strategies for doing your job well and making other contributions even as a culture misfit, that is, as someone who does not believe and/or behave as prescribed by the culture (Figure 5, page 19): self-insurance, cultural insurance, creating a counterculture, and creating culture change.

Strategy #1: Self-Insurance

Self-insurance means reliance on your relationships and credibility with the key players and others in the organization. The greater your culture misfit, and the more you deviate from the cultural norms, the more you will need their support.

Effective use of the self-insurance strategy over time requires that your performance and other contributions replenish your credibility.[6] If you can do this successfully over a period of time, you can acquire the reputation of "a respected misfit." Here is how Roderick Smallwood—the manager who chose to conform in terms of the cars he drove—did this:

Over the years, Smallwood had gone out on a limb to stake his reputation on business ideas that were culturally taboo—for example, fixed-price government contracts on which the company had lost a great deal of money in the past. Several of these counterculture projects that he championed eventually became big winners for the company. As his credibility grew, he continued to violate the cultural norms when he felt his business convictions, based on in-depth industry knowledge, justified it.

A certain amount of such nonconformity gradually became expected of Smallwood, and even after once engaging in insubordination, his credibility remained intact because so many of his nonconformist actions produced results that were highly valued by the organization.

Al Hirsch, the contrasting manager who did not give up driving his flashy European cars to work, also championed counterculture projects that he felt were in the organization's best interest. He, too, was replenishing his drained credit when some of his actions delivered high performance and other valuable contributions. However, Hirsch was using up more credit than Smallwood because he was further from the good soldier position (Figure 5, page 19) than was Smallwood.

Both Hirsch and Smallwood undertook initiatives that violated the cultural norms because they felt these moves were in the best interest of the organization. These *noble* nonconformists should be distinguished from the *arsonist* who violates the cultural norms to harm the organization.

Strategy #2: Cultural Insurance

The cultural insurance strategy calls for the support of the *powerful* good soldiers, thus spreading the risk of nonconformity among the "true believers" and the "old faithful" who have clout. For example, consider President James Hightower's actions at Atlantic Engineering. Hightower relied not only on his high credibility in the organization but also on the support of the company's two most powerful good soldiers—the board chairman and the corporate CEO. Their support enabled him to work through the inventory crisis by violating the cultural norm of "delegating" the problem upward (to these two powerful good soldiers) and helping his managers to solve the problem on their own instead.

Strategy #3: Creating a Counterculture

It is also possible to make contributions despite your misfit with an organization's culture by relying on the support of *less powerful* players, provided there are sufficient numbers of them. In the typical case of this strategy, the leader of an organizational subunit creates a culture that is counter to the company culture.

The classic case is of John Z. DeLorean at General Motors (GM).[7] The four core values at GM during DeLorean's tenure were respect for authority, fitting in, loyalty, and teamwork. DeLorean was able to create a counterculture by articulating opposing values, translating them into concrete policy, and facilitating their implementation by personally role modeling the counterculture values. Of course, the counterculture and its leader may not survive, just as DeLorean did not last at GM.

In general, it is difficult for such a counterculture to survive in the corporation unless the most powerful top executives support it. For example, the GM subsidiary Saturn was built from the ground up with an automobile manufacturing and industrial relations strategy radically different from that of the parent. It survived because it was the brainchild of the top brass, but the concept still failed to diffuse to the rest of GM.[8]

Strategy #4: Creating Culture Change

The organization's culture may need to be changed and brought into alignment with your own beliefs and values. If this is accomplished, you will not be a culture misfit anymore. This may be your explicit or implicit agenda as a leader who is trying to change the organization's culture (see Key #10).

Two Types of Conflict

If your plans for improving performance or making other contributions to the organization are opposed by others, you must manage the resulting conflict.

Conflict typically has two dimensions, one *task-related* and the other *emotional*. Task-related conflict arises from basic differences of opinion concerning what the organization should do, how it should do it, why the performance is what it is, and who should be held responsible for what. Emotional conflict arises from feelings of interpersonal rivalry, political threat, and hidden agendas.

Task-Related Conflict

One common variety of task-related conflict occurs between different functional departments within the organization. For example, the jobs to be performed by sales, research, and production are sufficiently distinct so that these departments are typically staffed with people having different backgrounds and predispositions, and these differences are further reinforced daily because the tasks demand different orientations toward goals, time frames for getting things done, and interpersonal requirements.[9]

Another common variety of task-related conflict is found between offices in different countries, and between these offices and the headquarters of multinational or multiregional organizations. Here the differences in national or regional cultures also have a lot to do with the latent or manifest conflict.

Yet another type of task-related conflict derives from a mismatch in personal values.[10] For example, Bob Drake's boss wanted him to fire an employee without giving him the two-weeks' notice per company policy, insisting that managers had the discretion to apply the policy as they saw fit. Bob disagreed and had to deal with the resulting task-related conflict with his boss. A similar example is the conflict among those who want to invest in people development because they are "the company's most valuable asset" and others who want to pay lip service to this value and eliminate or defer investments in education and training instead.

Emotional Conflict

Any action that seeks to alter the formal, social, or political system in the organization has the potential to upset some people and create emotional conflict. Emotional conflict may be hard to detect because the real reasons for the resistance may not be mentioned. The conflict may be couched in rational terms without acknowledging the perceived threat. Task-related issues may be emphasized, inflated, or even created in order to displace or mask the emotional ones. Opponents may argue that your plans or actions are inconsistent with the organization's culture, or the conflict may be attributed to "reasonable differences of opinion," posing it as task-related rather than as emotional conflict. Or the resistance may go underground and surface as opposition in some other form.

If the organization's culture encourages open dissent, conflict is more likely to be above board.[11] If not, it will be driven underground or the disagreements will be disguised in ways that are culturally acceptable. The conflict may then become manifest as lack of cooperation, passive resistance, or even sabotage. These situations are obviously more difficult to deal with.

Manage Both Types of Conflict

It is helpful to view resistance as an invitation to better understand yourself and others in order to reduce task-related and emotional conflict, and reframe it in win–win terms.

For example, President James Hightower at Atlantic Engineering experienced a conflict between the old guard and the new guard. Rather than taking sides and polarizing the conflict, Hightower engaged both groups in joint problem solving. Instead of conceptualizing the problem as "us" (new guard) versus "them" (old guard), he viewed it as a problem of mutual understanding. Hightower wanted to retain the pluses of the old guard and keep them with him. He succeeded by recognizing that there would be people on *both sides* who would see the inherent worth of what he was advocating and eventually would change but that some people on *both sides* wouldn't and they would have to leave. That is in fact what happened.

Emotional conflict is generally manifest as covert activities and actions. Their exact nature and form depend on the culture, the relative power of the opposing parties, and their values and ethics. The manifestations of the emotional conflict and the methods used to deal with it are limited only by the ingenuity and integrity of those involved.

Agendas of Opponents Who Feel Threatened, and Your Options

We will illustrate some of the personal agendas and the corresponding strategies and tactics that might be more or less covertly used by your opponents who feel threatened, and discuss some of the options available to you for dealing with them.[12]

Opponents' Agendas

When opponents feel threatened, one or more agendas may consciously or unconsciously emerge in their dealings with you. Several strategies may be used for each agenda, and various tactics are available to implement each strategy.

Agenda 1: Wear You Down

The strategy of flooding you with too much information may be implemented by the tactic of sending "pertinent" information extracted from thick reports and documents, which would take you time and energy to locate, analyze, and address.

A second strategy is to argue that you have provided too little information to make a convincing case. An aggravating tactic is to pester you with requests for additional details and clarifications that are peripheral to the salient issues.

A third strategy available to wear you down is to deflect you from the proposed course of action by raising other "more important" (but less threatening) issues that need to be dealt with. One tactic is to cite a previous study or to commission a new one in order to point out other issues that need more immediate attention. Another tactic is to get a committee (of one's supporters) to look into the question of "where best to deploy our limited resources." Where the opponent is in a hierarchically superior position, he or she may simply load you up with additional and allegedly more pressing assignments to deflect time and energy away from your proposed course of action.

Finally, the opponent may be able to wear you down by demeaning you. The tactics available are not acknowledging you or your contributions, or worse, taking credit for your accomplishments and ideas. An opponent in a superior position may also demean you by giving you assignments and amenities that deny or inadequately recognize your performance and other contributions to the organization.

Agenda 2: Destabilize You

The second basic agenda of opponents who feel threatened is to undermine you by pulling the rug out from under you. One strategy is to discredit you. A tactic employed is to make you look bad in the eyes of others, particularly those who are powerful. For example, one peer who felt threatened by the proposals of an up-and-coming rival began to send him memos (with copies to significant others, including their common boss), backdated so as to make it appear that the proponent was taking longer to respond than in fact he was.

Another destabilizing strategy is to lure you into a situation where you are likely to end up looking bad. A tactic is to give you an "once-in-a-lifetime" opportunity, such as a client or a customer who is in fact a can of worms, or the opportunity to make the opening or concluding presentation before a group that the opponent knows will shoot you down.

Agenda 3: Eliminate You

A third and final agenda of a threatened opponent is to try and eliminate you from the organization. One strategy for doing this is indirect intimidation. Tactics include attempts to nullify, isolate, and eventually ostracize you. A second strategy is direct intimidation.[13] One tactic is defamation by spreading rumors and gossip about you. Beyond rumor mongering, sinister planning by threatened opponents may include purposefully creating a negative image of you as inefficient or lacking in understanding, or making you a scapegoat, a whipping boy, or the butt of jokes.[14] Where the opponent can arrange it, another direct intimidation tactic is to seek your expulsion from the organization.

Your Options

You have three basic options to deal with these opponent agendas. For all three, it helps to understand the underlying reasons for the perceived threat and try to resolve it in as constructive a manner as possible.

Option 1: Use Reason and Appeal

This is the preferred option, if at all possible. One strategy of reason and appeal available to you is to win the opposition over. It might take some time to do this, and the persuasion, to be effective, might have to rely on both overt and covert tactics.

Another strategy is to seek intervention of a relatively neutral third party who is trusted by both sides. One manager got his boss two levels up to mediate a conflict with a peer in another department who also reported indirectly to the same boss. More formal third-party intervention may rely on a professional mediator, from either within or outside the organization.[15] For third-party intervention to work, however, the organization's culture must allow for an open airing of differences.

The win-the-opposition-over and the formal and informal intervention strategies work best in situations when there are only a few opponents. When the opponents are more numerous and the perceived threat more widespread, the strategy of moving incrementally may be used. Here you should move forward one step at a time, allowing consensus to build for your position along the way.

Option 2: Avoid the Opposition

A second basic option you have in dealing with the opposition is avoiding it. One strategy is for you to withdraw from the opponent's turf. A manager who was being intimidated by a seasoned organizational "shark" decided to seek a transfer to another division of the company to avoid this adversary who was trying to eliminate her. The argument for this tactic of survival is captured by the old saying, "He who fights and runs away lives to fight another day." The opportunity for doing what needs to be done is delayed to when something *can* be done.

The avoidance strategy may lower your credibility in the eyes of the opponent and others. It also raises ethical questions: If the opponent is harming the organization, is it OK to leave such an opponent unchecked? Is it ethical to leave the opponent free to prey on unsuspecting others? Both the pragmatic and the ethical difficulties indicate the importance of *how* you withdraw from the opponent's turf. The pragmatic difficulty may be addressed if you can withdraw without loss of face, perhaps even making it appear that the move is unrelated to the opponent's resistance. The ethical question may be dealt with more or less satisfactorily if you succeed in alerting those left behind to the ways of the opponent.

A second avoidance strategy is to ignore the opponents. If they cannot block you, and if you have sufficient credibility, you may be able to see the proposed action through. One problem with this is that the wear and tear on you may hurt your credibility.

A third avoidance strategy is to give in. Unless you have been persuaded that the opponent's resistance is in fact responsible behavior, the ethical questions this strategy raises are even more troublesome than avoidance by withdrawal. To use a religious metaphor, here you have joined the devil.

Option 3: Fight the Opposition

This option calls for the use of force in overcoming threatened opposition that is blocking you. One strategy is to openly confront the opponent; this was the approach taken by the manager who was being sent back-dated memos from a threatened rival. It can work if you have more credibility than your opponent.

A second strategy to fight the opposition is to use their arsenal. The pragmatic question here is whether or not it will work. For example, if you are new to the games of sabotage played by the opposition, you may lose. The ethical questions are: Do the ends justify the means? Can one condone this strategy on the basis that the other party is doing the same thing?

A third strategy is to build alliances. The key here is the aggregate credibility of your supporters versus that of the opposition. The major drawback of this approach is the amount of time it generally takes to build alliances. This difficulty diminishes when a coalition stabilizes around several issues and actions, forming a clique.

The use of force is an inherently unstable alternative in the long run. It breeds resentment, escalates tension higher on the conflict spiral, and eventually brings retaliation. However, if reason and appeal is not a viable option, your choice is either to avoid the opposition or to fight them. Each raises its own questions concerning effectiveness and ethics.

Summary

Key #9 first shows you how to improve your performance and make other contributions by leveraging the organization's culture. To do this, you must remain attuned to the culture, operate in a manner that is culturally acceptable, and acquire the necessary language (use of appropriate words and symbols) and argumentation skills.

There are four basic strategies for improving your job performance and making other valuable contributions to the organization even if you are a culture misfit, that is, even if you do not believe or behave as prescribed by the culture: self-insurance, cultural insurance, creating a counterculture, and creating culture change.

When your plans or actions to improve performance or make other contributions are opposed by others, it is important to distinguish between task-related and emotional conflict, and manage both constructively. If you are opposed by those who feel threatened, such opponents may try to wear you down, destabilize you, or eliminate you. If your attempts at reason and appeal fail, there are ways to avoid the opponents or to fight them head on in order to do what is right.

We turn next to Key #10, the contributions you can make by becoming a manager, a leader, and an entrepreneur.

Contribute by Becoming a Manager, a Leader, and an Entrepreneur

There is no God-given law that prevents you from becoming a manager *and* a leader *and* an entrepreneur—at any given time or over time. What you should do will depend on the needs of the organization, and what you are able to do will depend on your inclination, training, and skill.[1]

The organization's needs, and your personal background and inclination, may at first enable you to make one of these contributions more naturally than the others. But there will be many chances for you to make the other contributions later on. You should try to make all these contributions over time. This will help you to develop your skills and discover what you are really good at and what you like best as your career unfolds.

As Herminia Ibarra (2004, p. 163) concludes in her study of mid-career transitions (chapter 8, "Becoming Yourself"), "The most typical problem at mid[-]career is not defining what kind of work we find enjoyable and meaningful. Rather, it is figuring out how to transfer old preferences and values to new and different contexts[,] and how to integrate those with changing priorities and newly blooming potential."

Key #10 does not attempt to review the vast literature on managers, leaders, and entrepreneurs. It outlines some of the valued contributions and encourages you to make them.

Contribute by Becoming a Manager[2]

Peter Drucker defines a manager as someone who gets work done through others. To contribute valued results, a manager must get work done better, faster, and with fewer resources.[3] To do so, a manager must (1) plan and budget for the efficient use of resources; (2) abandon wasteful and unnecessary work; (3) ensure that all positions and hierarchical levels add value; (4) hire and retain the best person for each position; (5) ensure that everyone's skills, effort, and support match their job challenges; (6) unlock human potential via "self-control"; and (7) hold people accountable—not for the activities they perform in their jobs but for the results they produce.

Use Planning and Budgeting for the Efficient Use of Resources

In a fast-changing world, plans become obsolete soon after they are made. So why bother making plans? The answer is that good managers focus on *planning* rather than on the plan. They recognize that the principal benefit of planning, properly done, is in the discipline of thinking about what the organization's purpose and objectives are and how best to accomplish them over the next 1 to 3 years. With such preparation, it is then possible to respond effectively and quickly when changes occur.

Budgeting is the tool that managers use for the efficient allocation of the organization's resources. Too many organizations still use 12-month budgets, which is too long a horizon for today's pace of change. Ninety-day budgets are far more effective because the assumptions on which they are based are more likely to be valid. The bestseller *Execution* contains a useful discussion on budgeting for today's organizations.[4]

Abandon Wasteful and Unnecessary Work

"If you were not already in this business, would you enter it today?" is the famous question Peter Drucker asked Jack Welch when he took over at General Electric (GE). According to Welch, this simple question led him to reexamine GE's businesses, eventually leading to his own equally famous dictum to "fix, close, or sell" any business in which GE was not, and could not become, the #1 or #2 player in the world.

Drucker's simple but powerful notion of "abandonment" applies not only to businesses of a company but also to any work of an organization. ("If you were starting today, would you do it this way?") The reengineering movement that swept the world in the 1990s was based on this notion, with information technology offering a better way to get work done.

Jack Welch institutionalized the notion of abandonment by initiating the " workout" process at GE.[5] Every manager was required to meet with his or her people as long as necessary, typically for 2 to 3 days at a time, to examine how work was being done and how it could be done better if one started out with a clean sheet of paper. The manager's boss attended these workout sessions to observe and to advise, and an outside facilitator guided the structured process to ensure that everyone was heard and that every issue got on the table.

It takes courage and commitment to put the notion of abandonment into practice. Uprooting existing ways of doing things implies big changes in the formal, social, and political system of the organization. As discussed for Key #9, the resulting task-related and emotional conflicts can derail abandonment. GE's Welch said it took *5 years*[6] of repetitive workout sessions before substantial improvements were realized; without Welch's power and commitment pushing the process forward, workout would have failed as did many reengineering efforts that did not have a high-level champion.

Ensure That All Positions and Hierarchical Levels Add Value

Each position must add value. The "crossroads model" developed by GE and elaborated by Ram Charan, Stephen Drotter, and James Noel[7] emphasizes that each hierarchical level must add value as well (Figure 12). To accomplish this, a person's contributions must change dramatically as he or she is promoted from being an independent contributor (Manage Self) to manager (Manage Others) to managing those who manage others (Manager of Managers) and so on up to managing the entire enterprise (Enterprise Manager).

At each crossroad, the person being promoted must make the necessary "turn" by letting go of some of the contributions that made him or her successful in the prior position and learn new skills, adjust to a new time orientation, and adopt a new mindset in order to deliver the valued contributions in the new position.[8] Unfortunately, too many people fail to make the turn and continue instead along the line they were on in Figure 12, with old skills, old orientation, and old mindset—leading to the old contributions rather than the valued new ones.

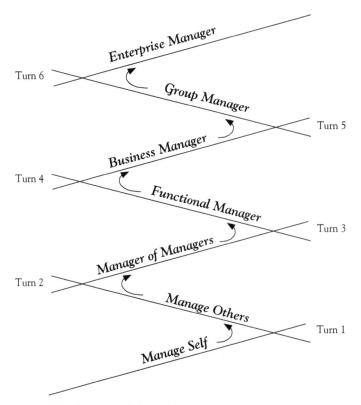

Figure 12 The "crossroads" model

Based on Charan, R., Drotter, S., & Noel, J. (2001). *The leadership pipeline: How to build the leadership-powered company* (Fig. 1, p. 7). San Francisco, CA: Jossey-Bass.

For an illustration based on the work of Charan, Drotter, and Noel, consider Turn #4 (Figure 12), which a functional manager must make when promoted to business manager.[9] The job challenges of the new position call for the following:

1. *New valued contributions.* Short-term financial performance and long-term business building.
2. *New skills.* Develop business strategy and business acumen, make trade-off decisions, and integrate the plans and programs of diverse functions into one effective business plan.
3. *A new time orientation.* Move easily from the here and now to 3 years out and back again; spend time working with functions perhaps not understood or valued in the past.

4. *New mindset.* Change mindset from a functional perspective ("can we do it?") to a profit perspective ("should we do this?"; e.g., "will we make money?").

The organization that a manager is responsible for should be designed with the aim of minimizing duplication and redundancy between positions and levels and maximizing the value added by every position and hierarchical level. But design alone will not be sufficient. Those making a "turn" need education and training to learn the new skills, adjust to the new orientation, and adopt the new mindset to make the new valued contributions. People also need coaching and some firms are offering it as a matter of policy to those who are making a "turn."

Hire and Retain the Best Person for Each Position

What could be more obvious than the need to hire the best person for each position? And yet it deserves special mention because this is generally not handled as well as it should be. As Claudio Fernandez-Araoz points out in his book *Great People Decisions*, "*the ability to make great people decisions is the most powerful contributor to career success.*"[10] Fernandez-Araoz not only explains why great people decisions matter so much and why they are so hard to make, but also provides practical guidance on how to appraise, attract, motivate, and integrate the best people.

Practical advice on identifying and retaining the best players for each position is included in the book *Topgrading* by Brad Smart and Geoff Smart.[11] The goal should be to find and retain "A players" (those in the top 10 percent of the talent available at a given salary level)[12] for at least the "A positions" (those which are strategically the most important),[13] and "A performance" should be expected from people in all positions.

Ensure That People's Skills, Effort, and the Support They Receive Match Their Job Challenges

Managers must ensure that their own skills, effort, and support match their job challenges, per Key #2 to deliver "A performance." They must also strive to make this happen for *every person* for whom they are responsible.

Research in progress indicates that newcomers typically feel anxious because their job challenges exceed their skills and support, but many established members report insufficient challenges, skills, and support, and feel apathy and boredom instead (Figure 7, page 27). This is a terrible waste in both economic and psychological terms that managers can prevent by ensuring that everyone has challenging work, develops the necessary skills, puts in the required effort, and receives the appropriate support to deliver "A performance" and derive job satisfaction, happiness at work, and personal and professional growth.

To accomplish this, a manager must have an organization designed with the right jobs; place the right people in all jobs; motivate them with the right incentives; provide valid and timely feedback to them on their performance; and educate, train, and coach them as required for them to excel.

Address the Special Needs and Challenges of Today's Workers

As Sandra Burud and Marie Tumolo point out, the traditional "breadwinner" of the past worked in a fairly stable job, in a fairly stable industry, full time, throughout a working life, and with a partner who managed family and home. In contrast, today's "dual-focus" workers (2004, p. 58) must manage work and personal life simultaneously. Today's typical worker is (2004, p. 52)

1. A person doing knowledge or service work in a highly competitive environment that relies on innovation and collective performance[;]
2. A worker with access to a variety of employment arrangements—apt to work as a contingent worker, interrupt a career, or work well beyond retirement age (probably part time) and receive some income from non-salary earnings[;]
3. A male or a female in a household where all adults work virtually full time with no full-time system of support at home. This makes a singular focus on work undesirable and often impossible.

A growing body of research strongly indicates that high-performance work practices (HPWPs) are better suited to the needs of today's workers and can boost their job performance, job satisfaction, happiness at work, and personal and professional growth.[14]

HPWPs may be usefully clustered as (a) family friendly work policies, including flexible hours and parental leave for child support; (b) human resource practices such as appropriate education and training and adequate incentives to induce attachment to the firm; and (c) design of work[15] to increase employee engagement by making work more meaningful for those performing it. While the specific practices vary, the evidence suggests that a well-integrated *system* of HPWPs creates better results than an ad hoc collection of best practices.[16]

You may not be in a position to implement HPWPs across the firm, but you can do your part to bring this opportunity to the attention of senior management, and also implement these practices within your zone of discretion to the extent possible. Today's workers for whom you are responsible seek HPWPs; respond to them with higher levels of job performance; and derive greater job satisfaction, happiness at work, and professional growth from using them.

Unlock Human Potential via "Self-Control"

Managers should strive for what Peter Drucker calls "self-control"[17]—a situation in which the people for whom a manager is responsible understand what needs to be done and why, and feel emotional ownership and accountability for getting it done.

Managers are accountable for the results that their people produce, so these results must be monitored and controlled. Good managers understand that monitoring involves the gathering of valid and timely information on performance—answering the question, "What are the results?"—and that the essence of "controlling results" is diagnosis and learning—"Why are results off-target and what needs to be done to achieve better results?"

If managers ask these questions and then give detailed instructions on what to do next, that is micromanagement. A good manager helps his or her people to understand what happened and why, and allows *them* to take corrective action and exercise self-control.[18]

Hold People Accountable for Results, Not Activities

People like to exercise self-control but they don't necessarily like the accountability for results that goes along with it. For self-control to work, managers must hold their people accountable—not for the activities they perform in their jobs but for the *results* they produce. What happens when managers hold their people accountable for performing activities rather than for delivering results? Naturally, the focus of their people then shifts to performing these activities rather than on taking ownership for finding new and better ways to deliver the best results.

Try the following exercise with the people who report directly to you. It works best in an interactive session with them led by you, with the help of a facilitator if you prefer. Write down what you are responsible and accountable for. Is it a list of activities or results? Ask your people to write down what they are responsible and accountable for. Is it a list of activities or results? It is not always easy to decide if an item is an activity or a result. A *group* discussion of several specific items from various participants, one by one, is typically necessary before the group gains clarity and consensus on whether an item is an activity or a result. Everyone can then review their lists and restate all items that are in fact activities by asking: What *results* are these activities supposed to deliver?

Valid and timely feedback to your people on whether or not they have achieved the stated results—and educating, training, coaching, and mentoring them—is critical for success.

Contribute by Becoming a Leader

The leadership literature can be grouped into three clusters according to whether the central focus is on: who leaders are, how they behave, or what they contribute. This book belongs to the third cluster because the focus is on what leaders *contribute*—that is, the valued results they deliver. One essential contribution is the creation of a vision that motivates and aligns employees and other stakeholders with the purpose and goals of the enterprise. A second valued contribution is the creation of necessary change to achieve this vision. We begin with a brief overview of a selection of the literature in the first two clusters—on who leaders are and how they behave.

Who Leaders Are

Over 30 years ago Abraham Zaleznik wrote a controversial article, "Managers and Leaders: Are They Different?" Zaleznik maintained that they are different and that leaders are born, not made.[19] This is not a popular view today but it is instructive to understand Zaleznik's argument for the personal insight it can offer.

His examples of leaders are drawn from the military and from entrepreneurial start-ups—that is, independent entrepreneurs rather than corporate leaders and corporate entrepreneurs—and he contrasts them with corporate managers. Zaleznik argues that leaders have an active attitude toward goals, not a passive attitude as managers do. In other words, leaders have a personal passion about the goals they pursue, whereas managers pursue goals that are assigned to them. Differences in conceptions of work follow. Leaders do not shy away from high-risk positions to achieve the goals they so passionately care about. Managers pay attention to process, conflict, and compromise to achieve the goals they have been assigned. The passionate pursuit of the goals they deeply care about drives leaders to take high-risk positions and gives them a feeling of separateness from others, which is why they have turbulent relationships with others. In contrast, managers experience a sense of belonging and have harmonious relationships with others.

Do these distinctions ring true? If yes, does it follow that leaders are "born, not made"? Individuals have natural inclinations, of course, but there is plenty of evidence that a lot also depends on people's life experiences and the situations they find themselves in.[20] A person may pursue his or her goals passively under one set of circumstances and pursue them passionately under different conditions.

So the real question for you is: are you closer to Zaleznik's leader or manager *for the work goals that you are currently pursuing*? Why? Test your response with someone who knows you well and will tell you truthfully. The resulting self-insight may give you a deeper understanding of who you are, what you are really passionate about, and your attitude toward the goals you are currently pursuing.

Good leaders have a moral compass that they use to guide their actions. They try to do the right thing and avoid the wrong shortcut. Three qualities good leaders share in common are integrity,[21] internal consistency, and authenticity. As former CEO Bill George of Medtronic states in his book, *Authentic Leadership*,[22] executives have learned to listen to every voice except their own. To become a leader, you need to listen to the voice within you.

In his best seller, *Good to Great*,[23] Jim Collins describes leaders at five different levels: individual contributors (Level 1), team members (Level 2), managers (Level 3), most leaders (Level 4), and leaders who build enduring organizational greatness with a paradoxical combination of humility and fierce resolve (Level 5). Using this scheme, at what level are you right now? What level of leadership do you aspire to?[24]

How Leaders Behave

John Kotter argues that managers and leaders behave differently.[25] Managers focus on planning and budgeting, organizing and staffing, and controlling people. In contrast, leaders give their people a sense of direction, align them with that direction, and motivate them by emphasizing intrinsic rewards. Kotter emphasizes the importance of leadership at all levels of the enterprise, not just at the top.

In her work on toxic leadership,[26] Jean Lipman-Blumen shows how people follow bad leaders such as Hitler in the political arena, and toxic leaders in the business hall of shame, because these leaders give their followers a sense of certainty, if not of destiny, that helps them to cope with their anxieties and fears. Rather than fostering this sense of dependence in the minds of their followers, good leaders help their people to grow and take responsibility for their actions.

What Leaders Contribute

Two important contributions leaders make are the creation of a compelling vision and the organizational change necessary to achieve it.

Vision

An essential valued contribution for leaders is a clear and compelling vision that motivates and aligns employees and other stakeholders with the purpose and goals of the enterprise.[27]

If you are leading a subunit of the enterprise—such as a team, a department, or a division—you can play your part in helping the organization to achieve and maintain a clear and compelling vision. Absent such a vision, you can help the organization to recognize its importance and contribute to its development. You can also provide your people a vision for your subunit that is fully aligned with the vision of your enterprise.

A bewildering variety of terms are used to describe vision—mission, values, philosophy, ideology, credo, and so on—and they mean different things to different people. It is more fruitful to ask these simple questions about vision:

1. *What* is the purpose of this enterprise and what are its goals?
2. *Why* does this enterprise exist? Why are its goals important to employees and other stakeholders?
3. *How* will the purpose and the goals be achieved?

In far too many companies, the answer to the "what" question about vision is "To be #1." But #1 in what? Market share? Service to clients? Profitability? Shareholder value? And even if the "what" is clear, why should employees and the other stakeholders care?

Most leaders prefer to focus on the "how" question about vision, which relates to strategy and execution. It *is* important, but a focus on "how" while ignoring the "why" is putting the cart before the horse. The horse is not going to go very far or very fast.

Ask most leaders *why* their enterprise exists and you get a blank look. After a moment's reflection, most business leaders, if they are honest, will say, "we exist to make money for shareholders." But as Peter Drucker warned over 50 years ago, profit is not an objective. Profit is necessary, but the purpose of the business enterprise is to create and serve a customer.[28] This lesson has been lost on the advocates of shareholder value, those who lead their enterprise with only the shareholder in mind, and the result has been Enronitis and the loss of credibility for business and its leaders.[29]

Edward Jones is a company that understands this important point. Its purpose is to offer sound financial advice to the serious long-term individual investor. The fact that Edward Jones is the highest performing company in an industry dominated by giants such as Merrill Lynch is the result of serving its customers better than anyone else; shareholder value is not the company's purpose. And in pursuit of the company's purpose, the employees (the financial advisors) derive a special sense of satisfaction from changing their customers' financial lives for the better. That is one reason why the company is routinely in the top ranks of *Fortune's 100 Best Companies to Work For* and other similar surveys of customer and employee satisfaction.

Vision Traps

Leaders can fall into one or more "vision traps," which prevent the development of a clear and compelling vision. The following are some examples of vision traps:

1. *Believing that visions can only come from the top.* GE's vision of becoming #1 or #2 came from CEO Jack Welch, but visions can also come from lower levels—not all wisdom is in the CEO's cranium. Intel's vision that it was a microprocessor company, not a memory chip company, came from the actions of its middle managers. Honda's vision of lightweight motorbikes for the American market was developed by its managers in the United States, not by Mr. Honda.

2. *Going to a visioning retreat and coming back with the answer.* As it has happened at many other companies, the top managers of Electromagnetic Systems Laboratory (ESL), a subsidiary of Thompson Ramo Wooldridge (TRW), went to a "visioning retreat" and came back with the answer, just as Moses came down from the mountaintop with the Ten Commandments! Unfortunately, unlike the words of Moses, the vision created by these top managers was neither clear nor compelling for the intended audience.

3. *Becoming obsessed with numbers.* Far too many leaders assume that a stretch target is their vision. For example, the vision of the ESL managers was the stretch target of reaching $1 billion in sales within 5 years. That was clear enough, but the "why" and the "how" questions regarding vision remained unanswered.

4. *Letting your need for growth drive your vision.* Top executives at Apple Computer in the early 1990s believed that the Newton, their pioneering personal digital assistant, had failed because "only" 140,000 units were sold in the first 2 years after introduction, versus the expectation of much higher sales. In contrast, Apple II, the company's pioneering personal computer, sold 43,000 units in its first 2 years

after introduction, but this was heralded as a great success![30] Why? Because a few million dollars of sales was seen as a great result when Apple was a start-up company and had no sales to speak of, whereas Newton had to become a billion-dollar business to be of any interest to the top executives of a 7-billion-dollar Apple Computer company.

There is an important lesson for leaders in this sad story—*the market does not care about your growth needs.* So it makes little sense to judge the success of a pioneering product based on a company's growth needs. Newton's "failure" to achieve its vision led to Palm Pilot's "success," and Palm Pilot *did* eventually become a billion-dollar success story.

Leaders Create Necessary Change

Another valued contribution for leaders is the creation of necessary change. I will describe five big mistakes leaders make when managing change and suggest ways to avoid these errors.

Mistake #1

The first mistake is the belief that to create change leaders must talk about it. But paradoxically, the best way to create change is to *not* talk about it. For talk about "change" often feeds people's fears and anxieties.

One business leader who failed in his change efforts put it this way: "What I talked about was the need to change. What my people heard is—he thinks there is something wrong with me." Let's face it. Although some people actually look forward to change, many others do not like it—even if there is a compelling need for change.[31]

Mistake #2

As the needs of the customers or other constituents change, the "theory of the business" may need to change also—which means that one or more shared beliefs and values may need to change or be reordered, but this is difficult because beliefs and values don't change easily (Key #1).

Leaders make their second mistake when they try to create change by attacking or blaming the organization's culture. You would do well to remember what too many leaders forget: if a shared belief or value exists, it *must* have served a useful purpose at one time, even if it has now become an impediment. An approach to change that honors the past while showing why the future demands something different is far more effective than the all-too-common approach of leaders who talk about what is "wrong" with the organization's culture and how (rather than *why*) it must be changed. Leaders would do better to ask themselves and their people the following question proposed by Roger Martin (1993, p. 88): what did we do *right* to get into this mess?

The popular advice to create a sense of crisis and a "burning platform" to get people to understand the need for change is just plain wrong. As Jim Collins points out, if leaders create a sense of crisis when there is none, they are being dishonest. Sooner or later people will see this and lose confidence and respect for their leaders, as well they should.[32]

Even if there is a genuine crisis, it is more productive to talk about what needs to be done rather than what is wrong. One of the greatest pieces of oratory in American history is Martin Luther King Jr.'s "I have a dream" speech, which appealed to the nation's sense of fairness, its constitution, and its highest ideals. What if King had given an "I have a nightmare" speech instead?[33] It would have strengthened the hand of racists and reactionaries who viewed the civil rights movement with fear.

To talk about what needs to be done, leaders must focus on the vision. Why does our enterprise exist? What are its goals? What are our results in comparison to our goals? Focusing everyone's attention on these simple, fundamental questions creates positive energy, even excitement, to get the organization moving in the right direction.[34] However, if they attack the organization's culture or focus on "change" as the objective, leaders obscure why change is necessary in the first place and generate negative energy instead.

A Higher Standard for Leaders. A higher standard for leaders, one that is missing in the writings on leadership, is the harnessing the full potential of the organization's culture, and its transformation when this is necessary. Three specific questions should be asked of every leader:

1. Could you have delivered better results, or delivered results more quickly, by harnessing the full potential of the organization's culture?

2. Did you help to remove the "cultural weeds" and the "poisonous roots" of the organization's culture—that is, did you modify or change the cultural beliefs and values that had outlived their usefulness or become dysfunctional?

3. Did you plant new "cultural seeds"—that is, did you embed new and beneficial cultural beliefs and values into the organization's culture?

Culture serves a function for leaders similar to that served by human genes for human beings. Culture perpetuates the values embedded by the leader. For example, William McKnight, who molded the culture of 3M Corporation, passed away long ago but his values concerning the importance of creativity and personal initiative live on in the 3M culture.

Mistake #3

A third mistake is the way in which some leaders develop a company's vision, mission, and values statements. Countless hours have been wasted in endless discussions and debates about what these terms really mean for the enterprise. The worst offenders dwell obsessively on getting the words just right, words that have a special meaning only for those who wrote them.

It is far more productive to conduct these important conversations with everyone connected with the enterprise (employees and other key stakeholders) "in English" and without buzzwords. Ask the three basic questions in commonsense words: *What* is the purpose of this enterprise? *Why* does it exist? *How* will we achieve its purpose?

If the people of the enterprise cannot give clear, compelling, and consistent answers to these simple, basic questions, the change process should aim to achieve this result because of the benefits for the enterprise, its employees, and other stakeholders:

1. *People with a sense of purpose.* Work is meaningful beyond the financial rewards.

2. *Intrinsic motivation.* There is energy, creativity, and excitement because people believe in the vision.

3. *Alignment.* Employees and other stakeholders are motivated and aligned with the aims of the enterprise.

Mistake #4

Leaders err when they focus on what their enterprise does not possess: "We do not have sufficient resources"; "We face powerful competitors"; "The government is a roadblock." The list of why something cannot be done is always long. But as several studies have demonstrated, it is not the lack of resources or a company's circumstances that prevent an enterprise from achieving its purpose. It is the lack of will to prevail over one's circumstances.[35]

Apple Computer did not have more resources than IBM in the 1970s when it pioneered personal computing, nor did it have more advantage than Sony and the other consumer electronics companies in the late 1990s when it created the iPod revolution in digital music.

Mistake #5

The final mistake concerns people—not listening to the skeptics and the cynics, not removing the change blockers, not hiring a critical mass of needed new blood, and not providing both education and training. Interested readers can refer to my article on this subject for an in-depth discussion; here are the main points.[36]

Listen to the Skeptics and the Cynics. Those who oppose change, including the powerful nonbelievers, must be given a chance to speak up. This is not only fair, it is also good business, because value can be derived from such opposition. Sometimes the proposed change is based on insufficient insight into the business and deserves to be challenged. At other times, people are skeptical because past failures have inoculated them against the need for change. Opportunities must be created for such skepticism and even cynicism to be openly aired and dealt with, for powerful nonbelievers can become evangelical supporters.

Remove Change Blockers. After good faith attempts at openness and fair play have been tried and after issues have been openly discussed and debated, there comes a time, about 6 months into the change process, when key people must be asked to either get on the train or get off. It is important to conduct this discussion with genuine respect for the differences of opinion that exist, especially in matters concerning vision, direction, and strategy, while at the same time emphasizing the need to have all the key people on board.

People who do not support the change must be identified and given an honorable exit (including a fair financial settlement). This may seem burdensome, but the cost is small compared to the cost of having powerful nonbelievers on board, who are likely to create a self-fulfilling prophecy by derailing the change process.

Strategically Hire a Critical Mass of Needed New Blood. The isolated hiring of outsiders has limited impact and runs the risk that the newcomers will become co-opted or neutralized by the established culture. But the strategic hiring of a critical mass of needed new blood can bring both the new minds and new behaviors required for change. These people can also serve as role models and coaches for insiders trying to change their mindset and behavior.

Provide Both Education and Training. Although many people use the terms "education" and "training" interchangeably, and the two are in fact related, there is an important distinction. Education imparts information and knowledge, and affects what goes on in the mind. Training imparts technique and skill, and impacts behavior more directly.

Lest this distinction seems academic, consider a practical example: Can one become a good golf player by simply reading, talking, watching, discussing, and understanding how the game is played? Education can impart information and knowledge about how golf is played, but one has to go out there and hit the little ball many, many times (preferably with the assistance of a coach) before one learns to play the game well. It is no different in the workplace. Leaders make the mistake of offering their people education only, training only, or worst of all, neither.[37]

Contribute by Becoming an Entrepreneur

When people talk about entrepreneurship they usually have an independent start-up in mind, where an individual or a group of individuals start a new business, a nonprofit, or a volunteer organization. But entrepreneurship is not limited to start-ups. It also occurs *within* established enterprises—private or public companies, government agencies, not-for-profit institutions, and volunteer organizations—when an individual or a group of individuals extend the scope of the enterprise with new products or new services, extend its reach into new markets, or create an entirely new business.[38] You can contribute as an entrepreneur both in a start-up and in an established enterprise.

Although entrepreneurship can occur in any setting, start-ups face challenges and require skills that are different from those necessary for entrepreneurship in an established enterprise. A start-up has no resources to begin with—financial, human, technical, or marketing—except those that the founders bring with them. The acquisition of new resources is thus a key challenge, and start-up entrepreneurs must have the skills to attract and retain both financial and human capital.

Entrepreneurs in an established enterprise face two very different challenges. First, an established enterprise has existing customers and established ways of serving them. Those pursuing a new business opportunity must overcome the organizational inertia of doing things in established ways. Second, though new resources are needed as in a start-up, an established enterprise has existing financial, human, technical, and marketing resources that can be *mobilized* in pursuit of a new business opportunity. This requires entrepreneurs who have the skill and the patience to build their relationships and credibility with the key players and others (Keys #3 and #4) and who can leverage the organization's culture and manage conflict (Key #9).

My book *Corporate Entrepreneurship* provides a detailed description of this phenomenon.[39] Here I will briefly describe three basic ingredients required for your survival and success as an independent or corporate entrepreneur.

Analogy to Crime: Means, Motive, and Opportunity

Both crime and entrepreneurship—whether independent or corporate—require the same three basic ingredients: means, motive, and opportunity! Entrepreneurs perceive new business opportunities, have the means to pursue them, and are motivated to do so. Let us consider each ingredient in turn, and the similarities and differences for independent versus corporate entrepreneurs.

Means

Some of the means necessary to pursue new business opportunities are the same for independent and corporate entrepreneurs: personal credibility in the eyes of the supporters, willingness to work with limited resources to achieve results, flexibility in responding to changing circumstances, and the ability to learn quickly as experience with the new venture accumulates.

But there are differences in the necessary means as well, which are clearly revealed when independent entrepreneurs join an established enterprise. One way this can happen is if an entrepreneurial firm is acquired by an established enterprise. If the acquired entrepreneur is allowed to run the business that he or she created with a great deal of autonomy and with little corporate interference, things can work well. But if the acquired entrepreneur is then given responsibility for a corporate new business in order to "inject entrepreneurship" into it, this rarely works.

The reason is that independent entrepreneurs typically have neither the skills nor the patience to develop their relationships and credibility with the key players (Keys #3 and #4), or to manage the culture and the politics of an established enterprise (Key #9), in order to build the required support for a new venture.

Motive

Some of the reasons why independent and corporate entrepreneurs pursue new business opportunities are the same (e.g., the satisfaction of creating a new product or service that creates value for customers and job opportunities for employees; the desire for industry and public recognition of one's achievements; the need to prove something to self or others).

Other reasons that motivate the two types of entrepreneurs are quite different. For independent entrepreneurs, important motivators are the desire to create an enterprise that they can leave to posterity, the opportunity for wealth creation, and the independence that comes with it. Corporate entrepreneurs know that they will not legally own what they create, that the financial rewards will be modest relative to those of independent entrepreneurship, and that they will have no enterprise to leave to posterity. But they might pursue new business opportunities because the culture values this or the boss expects it. If these motives dominate, and the entrepreneur is not motivated by a genuine commitment to the opportunity, there is the form but not the substance of entrepreneurship. Entrepreneurs—whether independent or corporate—must avoid such "fake entrepreneurship."

Opportunity

Firsthand knowledge of the business and a network of knowledgeable people with whom to test the new idea or concept are needed to identify the really attractive opportunities.

The independent entrepreneur can pursue any opportunity. The corporate entrepreneur must seek an opportunity that can be pursued advantageously given the resources and capabilities of his or her enterprise. If the opportunity of interest is entirely unconnected with the enterprise, it may be better to spin it out for independent pursuit.

Summary

Key #10 for creating a positive impact for your organization and yourself is the multiple contributions you can make by becoming a manager, a leader, and an entrepreneur. You may lean toward one of these contributions initially because of your background or training. But you should consider making the other contributions over time to help the organization and discover what you are good at and like best.

Managers deliver better results more quickly and with fewer resources because they plan and budget appropriately, abandon wasteful and unnecessary work, ensure that all positions and hierarchical levels add value, hire and retain the best person for each position, ensure that the skills and the effort of their people and the support they receive match their job challenges, unlock human potential via self-control, and hold people accountable—not for the activities they perform in their jobs but for the results they produce.

Leaders create a clear and compelling vision for their organization, and motivate and align employees and other stakeholders with the purpose and goals of the enterprise. They avoid vision traps. They also avoid the five mistakes commonly made in creating change, and leave the organization with new cultural seeds and in better shape than they found it.

Entrepreneurs pursue new business opportunities. Independent entrepreneurs face challenges that are quite different from those with which the corporate entrepreneurs must deal. But all entrepreneurs need the three basic ingredients for a successful "crime"—the means, the motive, and the opportunity.

You now know the 10 keys to survival and success in any job, in any organization, in any stage of the job cycle. I hope you will find them useful as your career progresses from one job to the next, whether in a start-up or an established for-profit, nonprofit, government, or volunteer organization.

PART V

How the Keys Work for Those Who Do Not Work in an Organization

Increasing numbers of people no longer work in an organization; they are what I call "solo operators." Anyone who works alone (without being employed by an organization and who is not an employer of others either) is a "solo operator" per this definition. Classic types of solo operators are independent entrepreneurs, consultants, and others who are neither employees nor employers. What if you are one of these solo operators? Can the 10 keys of this book be of any help to you?

As indicated in the opening passages of the introduction to this book, even if you are a solo operator, you probably deal with people who *do* work in organizations—they could be your customers, suppliers, or partners. You can better understand the challenges these people face in their jobs by viewing their situation through the lens of the 10 keys, and this will help you to deal with them more effectively.

You can also analyze your own situation by using these 10 keys—suitably modified to account for the fact that you are not formally employed by an organization—to improve your job performance, job satisfaction, happiness at work, and personal and professional growth. How such analysis can be conducted is illustrated next by Donna Finley, a solo operator *par excellence*.

Art by Jeffery Schidlowsky

Solo Operators

Reflections of a Solo Operator

by
Donna Finley

The solo operator is a challenging and rewarding way to channel a set of unique skills and appetite for change. As professionals mature through their career cycle, the opportunity to become a solo operator increases. However, experience is not the central component of this role, rather, internal drive, leadership acumen, and ability to adapt quickly and frequently are essential qualities for this career to succeed.

As there are many types of solo operators, I want to begin by describing the type of solo operator that I have been for the last 28 years. My background in brief is in the Appendix at the end of this chapter.

I have worked as a solo operator with organizations through a variety of different contractual arrangements. I have been brought in to help solve problems, and to navigate challenges and opportunities to take organizations to the next level of success. Typically, I lead a specific project, or a series of ongoing projects, while working closely with senior leadership, managers, and employees of the organization to develop strategy, plan, and assist through the implementation effort. Rather than prescribing "solutions," I guide the organization through rigorous internal and external analysis to arrive at mutually agreed-upon strategic options to pursue. Following this work, I may or may not continue working with the organization—whether on the current project or on an ongoing basis on future projects. I am expected to provide expertise, leadership, and objectivity, while assisting with the work. This is at the heart of what I do as a solo operator.

Comparison to Entrepreneurs

The main difference between my work as a solo operator and that of the classic entrepreneur is in the purpose behind the work. Entrepreneurs work on their own endeavors; I adopt and work on projects within organizations owned by others. However, like the classic solo entrepreneur, I also feel personally invested in the success of the venture, capped only by the duration of the relationship.

My type of solo operator and the classic entrepreneur share some characteristics. We are tenacious individuals who see each step along the way as an opportunity to hone abilities based on our previous experience. We are risk takers who are motivated by challenges. We are creative thinkers, who build forward on previous solutions. We are personally invested in the success of our clients, yet we are professionals who use the freedom and flexibility to shape our work and schedules each day. We pursue work that aligns with our evolving interests, skills, values, and passions.

However, some characteristics distinguish my type of solo operator from the classic entrepreneur. While an entrepreneur builds an organization around his or her dream, product, or service, a solo operator builds a community. An entrepreneur's energy is inward, directed to building an organization: hiring people and directing all aspects of the business (marketing, human resources, project management, design). They are exclusively dedicated to the organization they create and reap all of the residual rewards of the business effort.

In contrast, my type of solo operator accumulates knowledge without traditional asset creation. My energy is spread outwards, generating income by contracting myself out over and over, creating value where none had previously existed. Through this process, I develop a particular set of skills and resources, and generate revenue by expanding my business network over time.

Comparison to Consultants

While my type of solo operator shares many common characteristics with traditional consultants,[1] the primary difference is the type of engagement.

---

[1] Consultant: a person who gives professional advice or services to companies for a fee (www.merriam-webster.com).

The collaboration I require for my approach is at the upper end of the scale of involvement with employees of the host organization. Continued involvement with an organization could include periodic engagements, as required, resembling short-term employment. This depends on the needs of the organization, the scope of responsibility, and the duration of the project. Although one may have significant expertise in a wide array of business or technical fields, my type of solo operator does not necessarily embark on projects to impart their wisdom onto the organization; but rather to guide the organization through the work, driving the process, building knowledge capacity in teams, and mentoring senior leaders. Moreover, my work focuses on discovering root causes of barriers and resolving unforeseen issues along the way. In this way, my type of solo operator looks and acts much more like an employee or senior manager than an external consultant. Very simply put, a solo operator "lends a hand" albeit a very experienced hand versus bringing in a particular solution.

What Has Worked for Me as a Solo Operator

I am typically hired into organizations that have problems to solve, requiring strengths unavailable in-house, in conjunction with objectivity and a fresh perspective. I have no vested interest in any particular answer because I am an outsider who is independent of the internal politics, systems, and processes that have been built by others. I have also served in the capacity of an "in and out" leader, periodically providing mentorship, advice, and "course adjustments" over several years. To be effective, I have found a number of conditions to be critical.

Lead From Behind

It is important for me to "lead from behind" by seeking out senior managers and employees who are knowledgeable, thoughtful, well intentioned, and influential. Through a careful vetting process and various conversations supported by these leaders, it is possible to surface facts and internal perspectives that allow the organization to learn, and derive new insights and conclusions. My type of solo operator can provide organizations a great service by giving a voice to those who think they don't have a say or are not usually heard. This may sound rudimentary; however, this work is never easy. It is a calling for which I have endured many sleepless nights, as this voice is often not welcomed by entrenched management teams yet is an important part of the solution and needs to be considered. By the time I arrive, the situation has often deteriorated so much that people are refusing to talk to one another and the deadlock is well entrenched.

Challenge Traditional Assumptions

Deadlock can be accompanied by disagreements and strategic paralysis. In such an environment, people need to feel safe to speak and to know all perspectives are relevant and valuable. The immediate goal is to ensure that important decisions are made to guide continued healthy business operations and customer service. To move forward from such a point, the process can be arduous, yet very rewarding. By listening generously to the content as well as by feeling the emotion behind the words, I take copious notes, often writing down the exact words used in the discussion. I reflect upon what I have seen within the organization as well as outside the organization, in its context. I subsequently synthesize what I have heard, seen, and felt into images, ensuring objectivity. Unfortunately, this candid perspective is not always welcomed, making it not uncommon for managers to perceive me as directive. In reality, I am suggesting alternate courses of action they had not considered and am waiting for them to take a clear stance one way or another.

Leverage Experience Into New Contexts

On a personal level, the work of my type of sole operator is infinitely rewarding, stimulating creativity and interest in the work. I leverage a wealth of experience from multiple sectors and types of organizations and multiply its effects. This enables the host organization to benefit from an injection of innovative thinking that has proven successful elsewhere. Without the shackles of day-to-day busy work, my type of sole operator can focus their energies more directly, and aid organizations in new ways of thinking without increasing the head count. In turn, the host organization increases its functionality and professionalism, as it benefits from a new, committed, expert-employee who brings in new processes and constructs to quickly elevate the abilities and performance of employees.

When these observations and processes are embraced by management, the results and impact on business and employees can be profound.

Characteristics of an Ideal Host Organization

Inviting in a temporary senior expert-employee requires a host organization that has an appetite for change and a willingness to employ new ways of working. To most efficiently benefit from our partnership, the organization should possess advanced skills in leadership (of which there can be many styles) and the desire to lead, while at the same time maintain a mentality/predisposition to serve, guide, educate, and in some cases, nurture. Ultimately, however, success is measured through the relationship, especially the level of respect and trust attained. The evidence of a successful, strong relationship can be an invitation to work with the organization again. In fact, a good portion of my work is by word-of-mouth referrals.

What Does Not Work

A lack of support from the host organization in terms of leader involvement/commitment can be destructive to my work. A lukewarm senior leadership team and/or Board or a heavy-handed "my way or the highway" attitude will not positively affect the organization, rendering the candid perspective of the solo operator inconsequential. A recent project with a provincial human services agency supporting youth illustrates the effects of a lukewarm commitment. The original proposal called for a task team of three senior leaders to work collaboratively with my team. After just two months, only one director remained involved, who then was unable to effectively communicate key changes required within the organization to her peers. This resulted in more gridlock, misunderstandings, and lack of leadership, with several recommendations being discounted as simply "not relevant."

Similarly, a lack of commitment for the project or thoroughness by the sole operator will yield comparable results.

Although the sole operator may have the best of intentions for moving an organization toward success, the credibility of the solo operator and buy-in by the host organization must be established and maintained. Once a project is secured, a steep learning curve exists for the solo operator, for each and every project. This learning curve is frequently aggravated by timelines, purposely made short if financial, Board, or external pressures are extremely pressing. As one successful example, I was invited to facilitate a process to increase Jewish student enrolment in local Jewish day schools despite being outside that faith and culture.

Keys to Success

When I enter a situation, I have been hired to create a new way. I'm an outsider. I rock the boat because I challenge traditional assumptions, established rules and paradigms, which often disturb the status quo as well as the leaders who are working to maintain that status quo. Consequently, I need to have great faith in myself and quickly build trust in others. At times I have heard things like, "Your style is aggressive"; or "You drive too hard." However, on the other side I hear: "How did you see that so clearly?" and "How did you put that together?" To be my type of solo operator, you need to have desire to serve, self-confidence, belief in your methods, and the ability to, "Keep your head when all about you are losing theirs," as Rudyard Kipling said.

One particular case stands out in my career. In my final presentation to a consortium of three provincial government departments, I was questioned and accused by the Chair of not understanding or being aware of the organization's mission and objectives in front of 25 people. Taking a deep breath, I confidently gave a clear and concise summary of their mission and how my recommendations aligned to advance their purpose. Following the storm, three independent community members approached me to quietly confirm their support of my stance.

Upon reflection, there are several ingredients to success for my type of sole operator. These characteristics include the ability to learn and adapt quickly, drawing upon past experience and reservoir of knowledge and applying it creatively. Teamwork and an aptitude to "work and play well with others" are also necessary for my type of solo operator, as we constantly seek to support and foster leadership in others. Accompanied with trust, these traits build capacity in the host organization leading to a higher level of performance.

I said earlier that "success is measured by relationships" in regard to organizations. This same rule applies to my type of sole operator. Bonding with key leadership and employees is critical.

I always identify and nurture "anchors" (i.e., influential leaders) within an organization who give me the credibility I need to build trust with others. For example, my key anchor in a major transformation at the University of Calgary was a renowned traditional scientist and vice president of the university's administration. This highly regarded and credible academic helped to translate and transfer knowledge, and pave the way for acceptance of major changes proposed by an outsider (me and my team).

Externally, I rely on key mentors to help me maintain confidence in my leadership style and to remind me of my strengths. These people are essential supports that encourage me, challenge me, and offer me ideas and strategies.

The Theory of Success for a Solo Operator

Shifting our focus back to the 10 keys outlined in this book, all are important to my type of solo operator but how they are used will vary from one solo operator to another. How each key generally works for me is described in Figure 13.

In conclusion, being a sole operator has been extremely rewarding, despite the challenges described. It has required assertiveness, confidence, and strong leadership, alongside humility, empathy, and compassion. At times, projects have kept me awake at night, as I became part of the gridlock, fearing I may be creating more animosity than solutions. This is where a sole operator like me must exude self-confidence, dig deep, and listen, feel, and stick to his or her gut, knowing that if I weather the storm, the rain will bring sun. Being a sole operator of my type provides flexibility, and a freedom to choose projects that align with my values and evolving interests. With the variety of experience and exposure come numerous career and project opportunities such as Board work, senior management roles, and community leadership.

Key	How each key generally works for me
Key #4: Your credibility The higher your incoming **credibility** in the organization when accepting a new project, and …	• Credibility is what distinguishes me from other competitive alternatives being considered by the hiring team. • It directly affects my ability to lead and quickly engage participants.
Keys #5 and #6: Determine your gaps *prior to* accepting a new project The better the **diagnosis** that you have conducted prior to accepting a new project, and …	• "Fit" is critical to developing trust with the organization, understanding organizational values and project requirements, and assessing the skills and capabilities of assigned team members. • I try to get the following questions answered before accepting a new project: Do I need to augment my own team with additional subject matter experts (SMEs)? Do I need to incorporate additional market research? Is a critical date driving the project timeline? Is this a collaborative organization? • I assess organizational commitment to making hard decisions and the sophistication of their planning processes and experiences. • I look for their willingness to learn and change what they do and how they do it including organizations outside your sector. • I want to understand their budget expectations and restrictions because this indicates the scope of the project and resources the organization is willing to commit to for this work. I will adjust my scope and resources accordingly. • I try to identify a clear, influential leader supporting the endeavor and to ascertain the degree of his or her credibility within the organization. This person will act as a key translator between the organization and me, as needed changes are identified, and help to provide resources as well as remove barriers. This person will remain in the organization influencing implementation long after I leave. • I research who the organization has used before for planning support and the reasons why or why not that effort was successful. I ask, why aren't they using that consultant for this effort? • I determine who the decision-makers are for the work: Who has the "final" say? Who would I be reporting to? Who are the key individuals and groups I will have to persuade? How does one go about selling a new idea in this organization? • I determine if the project lead has a previous connection with a leader I have worked with (word of mouth). • I determine if I am the best fit for the work or if one of my business partners is a better fit for the engagement.
The more you have avoided the **traps** that derail the recruiting process, and …	How I deal with traps under the organization's control: • Language code: I use words carefully to describe my intentions. • Organizational oversell: Typically, the organization has less information about markets and about customers than is required, and what they do have is not always helpful.

Figure 13 The theory of success: How each key generally works for me

Key	How each key generally works for me
	• Organizational seduction: They often tell me: "You are a recognized SME!" But then they ignore my advice when the going gets tough or the change I am recommending is too great for them! • Homosocial reproduction: I do not fit well in "macho" companies. Since I am a female, I am perceived to be collaborative, which I am, but I am also confident, analytical, and candid, and the organization often finds it difficult to deal with this. • Interviewer's agenda: Sometimes it is difficult to determine if the organization is looking for me to justify the position they have already taken or if they are open to new thinking. How I deal with traps under my control: • I try to avoid self-seduction by inquiring about the potential organization through my peer network: What are they like to work with? How committed to change are they? How is decision-making conducted within the organization? Who have they worked with in the past? Why or why not did this work? • Also, I evaluate who else is being considered for my role (the short-listed competition).
Key #1: Your fit with the key players and the organization's culture The lower your misfit (gap) with your key players and with the organization's culture, and ...	• Directly affects my ability to lead and quickly engage participants, while challenging traditional assumptions held by the organization.
Key #2: Your project challenges versus your skills, effort, and support The lower your misfit (gap) with the skills, effort, and support that you will require to successfully address your project challenges, and ...	• I rely on specific technical aspects of the work being provided by the organization and/or on SMEs who I identify and bring onto the project team. • I must quickly climb a steep learning curve related to the sector in which the organization operates. • Directly affects my ability to lead and quickly engage participants, while challenging traditional assumptions held by the organization.
Keys #7 and #8: Talk less and listen more for effective onboarding The better your onboarding into the organization, and ...	• I try to listen and talk to convince the organization of what needs to be looked at. • I try to identify and listen to influential employees (may be positive or negative influencers) in confidential interviews I conduct as soon as possible and extend a bridge to those individuals. • I find the hidden, minority voices in the organization via confidential interviews as well. • I begin to develop a glossary of terms used within the organization and write them down explicitly.

Figure 13 The theory of success: How each key generally works for me (Contd.)

Key	How each key generally works for me
	• I conduct a situation assessment (key sector trends, competitive benchmarking, internal assessment via confidential one-on-one interviews, strengths and weaknesses of the organization, articulate problem to be addressed) and test the findings with the project team (and others). • I re-evaluate (and re-negotiate) expectations, scope, and timelines for the project in light of the information gleaned above. • I come with a set of frameworks and processes to guide the work. • I rely on specific technical aspects of the work being provided by the organization and/or on SMEs who I identify and bring onto the project team. • Onboarding is typically a matter of 1 to 2 weeks in a project; consequently, I do not typically have 12 to 18 months to develop good relationships. • I also have a responsibility to onboard the client, introducing him or her to the process and collaborative approach to co-creating solutions. This tends to be a significant collaborative learning for the organization. • I must remain objective. • I must rely on my "anchor" to privately test ideas, perceptions, personalities, hot buttons, and terminology. • I incorporate feedback into every working session so that barriers and concerns can be identified and addressed early in the process. • I may be brought into an organization to change some aspect of the culture; consequently, I am not always concerned about my "cultural fit" with the organization.
Key #3: Quality of your relationships with the key players and others The better your development of relationships with your key players and others in order to bridge the values gap with them and with the organization's culture, and ...	• I identify and nurture "anchors" (i.e., influential leaders) within the organization that give me the credibility needed to build trust quickly with others. • I must be able to read between the lines and sense emotions.
The greater the improvement in your skills, effort, and support to close the gap with what is required to successfully address your project challenges, and ...	• I come with a set of frameworks and processes to guide the work. • I rely on "anchors" to assist in the framing and interpretation of work and on specific technical aspects of the work being provided by the organization.
Key #9: Leveraging organizational culture and managing conflict The better your results and the greater your other contributions to your organization as an individual contributor, and ...	• I contribute to the work in a collaborative team effort. • To challenge and push thinking forward, I must be a master facilitator and resolve conflict.

Figure 13 The theory of success: How each key generally works for me (Contd.)

Key	How each key generally works for me
Key #10: Contributing as a leader, as a manager, and as an entrepreneur As a leader, a manager, and an entrepreneur, …	• My leadership role is important to the success of driving a project forward while gaining the trust and support of the organization. • I contribute to the work in a collaborative team effort, building capacity in leaders who will remain in the organization after I leave.
Key #4: Your credibility The more your credibility will grow in the organization—feedback loop to your credibility when accepting a new project.	• My credibility is critical to developing trust with the organization and matching my interests and passions. • Innovation occurs because I challenge the organization to push thinking forward.

Figure 13 The theory of success: How each key generally works for me

Appendix: My Background

Prior to becoming a solo operator, I was initially employed in a corporation, during which I changed jobs frequently in my first 5 years. Endeavoring to seek ever greater challenges, I held numerous positions, which ultimately provided me with experience in different aspects of management. I learned how to identify key messages and write speeches for senior executives as a communications specialist. I set up an integrated medical filing system for 15 companies as assistant to the vice president. I developed fitness and health protocols for senior executives as a research assistant in Occupational Health and Safety. I developed policies and procedures for the newly constructed corporate fitness center for 4,000 members.

I transitioned to the Computer Services Department to develop policy and procedures for larger systems and more money. I supported the vice chairman of the chemical division as his executive assistant. And, finally, I entered the marketing department as a marketing analyst, tracking and evolving the strategy for high-density polyethylene.

After this 5-year stint, I came to the realization that I needed to acquire deeper academic knowledge, in order to put my experience in context and prepare myself for more complex situations. I moved to Switzerland to attain by MBA. Diploma in hand, my first job as a sole operator was as a marketing coordinator for Hewlett-Packard, followed a year later by senior strategic planner at NOVA Corporation.

As a proven strategist with over 30-year experience, I have led several high-profile transformations. Most notably, my work of restructuring the Calgary Philharmonic Orchestra while in bankruptcy protection earned a National Award of Distinction. I am a strong advocate for mentoring youth, and have founded Connections—Women in Business Round Table, to help young women succeed in business. After selling the management consulting business I started 25 years ago, I now operate solo.

I value my Certified Management Consultant credential. I took time out from my busy practice to undertake and compete, in 2012, an interdisciplinary PhD at the University of Calgary. My doctoral research focused on developing new tools for transferring knowledge and building organizational and leadership capacity. I am the author of multiple academic articles and co-author of a textbook on strategic planning. I have been a keynote speaker on topics such as leadership, strategic planning, change management, and knowledge management. And I have been a guest lecturer at The Peter F. Drucker and Masatoshi Ito Graduate School of Management. All of this has helped me to become a more reflective practitioner, and hence a more effective one.

PART VI

Secret Sauce for Career Success

How will you measure your career success? Indeed, how will you measure your life?

In the short video on the link below, Clay Christensen tells us how he thinks God will measure his life and, whether we believe in God or not, invites us to ask: How will I measure my life?

http://www.youtube.com/watch?v=tvos4nORf_Y

You can watch the most pertinent segments of this 20-minute video in 7 minutes by starting at 7:50 minutes and viewing till 11:50 (4 min), then skipping to 16:50 and viewing till 19:50 (3 min).

So how *will* you measure your life? The answer is well beyond the scope of this book but it will influence how you answer the next question, which *is* central to this book: How will you measure your career success? What is your primary yardstick? Is it your career advancement or your contribution to others? Peter Drucker argued that it should be the latter because this leads to the most personally meaningful career. As pointed out in this book in the section "The Power of Calling" under Key #2, Abraham Maslow came to a very similar profound conclusion that "self-actualizing people are involved in a cause *outside* their own skin."

There is no inevitable conflict between your career advancement and your contribution to others, but what you focus on is crucial—a focus on advancement may not lead to contribution, but a focus on contribution will more likely lead to the advancement.

In my view, contribution to others *is* the path to career success! And, as clearly spelled out in the Introduction under the discussion of Figure 1, my definition of success is results that benefit both self and others.

If that is also your definition of success, then I would like to share with you my "secret sauce" for career success. My "recipe" is based on 30 years of teaching the course that led to this book. I have given this "secret sauce" to the participants at the end of my course, and the positive feedback that I have received leads me to offer it to you.

If you wish to use this "recipe," copy and paste it in a place that only you can easily see each and every day at work. And say to yourself as you read this:

"The secret sauce is my *mindset* and *behavior* each and every day at work:

1. I do excellent work, no matter how boring it may be. Excellence leads to professional pride and passion, and not just the other way around.
2. My managers or HR staff are *not* responsible for my career. I am.
3. I blame no one. I don't judge others or expect them to behave as I think they should.
4. I work hard to do a better job than my clients, managers, and coworkers expect—even if I am not fairly compensated for the work I do.
5. I don't let my ego or emotion get in the way of delivering outstanding results for my clients, managers, and coworkers—even if some of them can be unsupportive, unprofessional or rude, or are *not* nice people.
6. I play the role. If the workplace is a drama, I play my part with a thick skin rather than hoping for the perfect workplace.
7. I call a trusted advisor to talk about anything that does not go well at work, and about things that are going well."

People who have used this recipe tell me that it looks deceptively simple. It is, in fact, very hard to do this day in and day out. Success is not assured, of course, but this recipe may help you to improve your job performance, job satisfaction, happiness at work, and personal and professional growth.

Good luck, and all the best for a successful career ahead!

APPENDIX 1

Template for Self-Reflection

In my course for which this book is the text, students write a self-reflection paper as the final exam using a template that I provide. I grade the papers "blind" so the student name is included on a separate sheet at the back of the paper. Fictitious names instead of real names are used throughout the paper for any person or other entity mentioned in the paper.

The key requirements are (a) to pick a specific point in time at which the critical self-reflection will be performed using the 10 keys in this book, and (b) instead of the typical essay, the student must conduct a critical self-examination using the template that I provide to ensure that the relevant concepts and frameworks in the book are used to perform the required analysis.

The template consists of eight pages, typewritten and double spaced, and each question or item on it in **bold** letters must be answered by performing the required analysis in the space provided. Although students initially do not like the page and space restrictions imposed by the template and the analysis it demands, they later come to appreciate the insights that such a disciplined self-examination can yield. As Winston Churchill wrote at the end of a long letter to a friend: "I am sorry I wrote such a long letter. I did not have sufficient time to write a short letter."

A recent paper written by James Pike is included below with his permission. All other names in the paper are fictitious. It is a model paper that illustrates how you can answer the specific questions asked to conduct this self-reflection exercise for yourself using the template.

Model Paper Using the Template for Self-Reflection

by
James Pike

Page 1

Description of job, company, your key players, and time period for analysis (one short paragraph).

In 2009, I began working as a senior manager for Northwestern Research Institute (NRI). The institute conducted government-funded research on environmental, health, and safety issues. My role involved the oversight of logistical operations for these projects. Between January 1, 2012 and December 31, 2013, I reported to Dr. Tim Flanders—a respected researcher who had developed a new health program designed to assist low-income families. The other key players I relied upon were Dr. Malcolm Jackson, the director of the institute, Sally Bell, a research assistant with expertise in data analysis, and Jeanette Romero, a research assistant with prior experience in community outreach.

Evaluate job performance and only *one* other outcome (job satisfaction, happiness at work, personal and professional growth) on a scale of 1 to 9.

During this time period, I would give my job performance a 7 and my job satisfaction a 3.

Specify your evaluation criteria and make sure they refer to results (outcomes) and not inputs.

During annual performance reviews, Flanders evaluated my job performance based on the extent to which I could deliver high-quality datasets using minimal resources and by the degree to which I facilitated the production of scientific reports and publications. I assessed my job satisfaction by evaluating the freedom I was given to implement cost-cutting strategies and by the opportunities I had to collaborate with and learn from experts in the field.

Page 2

KEY #1: Cite evidence to support your analysis.

The success of NRI is largely determined by its ability to attract and retain experienced research personnel. As a result, a dominant value is that stressful, interpersonal conflicts must be minimized to prevent individuals from leaving the organization. A secondary value is that research must be conducted at the highest level of quality given the resources available.

For the dominant value, Tim Flanders would be classified as a good solider. In group meetings, he frequently espoused the need to create a hospitable work environment. When a personal conflict did arise between two employees, he quickly implemented a new reporting structure that eliminated interaction between these two individuals. Flanders also exhibited the traits of a good soldier on the secondary value. During budget reviews, he made sure that all surplus funds were allocated to new substudies that would lead to innovative scientific manuscripts.

For the secondary value, I would be classified as a good solider at NRI. This is evident from the fact that I frequently suggested and implemented cost-cutting measures for existing research operations so that additional sub-studies could be conducted. In contrast, I would be classified as an adapter on the dominant value. For example, I often coordinated group meetings where employees could discuss their opinions and concerns. However, when given a choice between conducting high-quality research operations and keeping the workplace relaxed and cordial, I chose the former. Consequently, I was a slight misfit with both the culture of NRI and Flanders, my immediate supervisor.

Page 3

KEY #2: Cite evidence to support your analysis.

My experience at NRI fluctuated between a state of anxiety and flow. On a technical level, the main challenge I confronted was that few systems had been developed for the type of research that was now being conducted. Fortunately, I had the opportunity to develop these systems on past projects I had managed. Thus, my overall experience in this area was close to flow. As for the industry, the primary challenge I faced was the amount of time it took to develop scientific manuscripts that required input from multiple co-authors. However, I had prior experience overseeing these types of collaborations so I felt comfortable with this aspect of my work. From an organizational standpoint, the greatest challenge was the misfit with my boss. Often, the solutions I proposed to a given problem would be delayed until they had been reviewed by all parties that might find them objectionable. As a consequence, the timeline for ongoing research operations was frequently delayed. I addressed this challenge by relying upon my technical knowledge to increase the pace of operations, but this often left me in a state of high anxiety.

While serving at NRI, I viewed my work as a calling. I firmly believe that new scientific insights have the power to dramatically benefit the public and should therefore be given top priority. Yet, my work often felt thwarted by the lack of systems available at NRI. Moreover, the support I received from Flanders was minimal as he did not want me to push other individuals to create new systems or provide services outside their normal milieu. I was able to partially address this problem by tapping into a large network of innovative and enthusiastic research assistants with novel solutions to the issues confronted by the project.

Page 4
KEY #3: Cite evidence to support your analysis.
The quality of my relationship with my boss was mixed. Some of Flanders' expectations were clearly described in the original research plan he had authored. Other expectations, such as his desire to only review fiscal issues when an emergency arose, took time to discover.

In terms of trust, Flanders had great faith in my reliability and my discretion. He never questioned whether I would be able to reach a stated deadline. He was also willing to share his personal insights on organizational changes that affected the future of NRI. In addition, Flanders sought my advice on how to best collaborate with other researchers on joint publications. Thus, he had a high opinion of my industry-related competence. Yet, Flanders also had doubts about my openness, intentions, and integrity. He knew that prior to working for him I had spent several years managing research projects for Jackson, the director of the institute.

Consequently, he suspected that I withheld information I acquired from chats I still had with Jackson. During one-on-one meetings, Flanders also made sure to delineate which of his statements may be shared with other researchers at NRI and which should be kept confidential.

As for influence, I had no formal authority over Flanders. However, I did have several personal bases of power. During the 2 years I worked with Flanders I developed many of the systems that became commonplace at NRI. As such, I was viewed as an expert in these areas and was asked by Flanders to serve as a consultant on other projects he was developing. I also had access to the opinions of his colleagues, such as Jackson, as well as a network of research assistants who were vital to research operations and manuscript development at NRI.

Page 5

KEY #4: Your *credibility* in the eyes of the key players.

In the eyes of Flanders, my credibility was average. On one hand, he valued my skills, contacts, and expertise. This became apparent during annual reviews in which my performance in these areas was consistently given an 8 or 9 on a scale of 1 to 10. He also frequently stated that my contributions were vital to the success of the program he had designed. On the other hand, Flanders was aware that I disagreed with his approach to managing personnel. He also recognized that I was a much closer fit to Jackson, who was an adapter on the dominant value and a good soldier on the secondary value. Accordingly, the credibility I gained was lessened by my misfit with Flanders and my own inability to overcome this gap in our relationship.

What drives *your job performance?*

My ability to deliver quality datasets was primarily driven by Keys #2 and #3. Using the skills I acquired on past projects and the relationships I developed with key research assistants, I was able to create a subculture unlike others at NRI. A good example of this is the fact that the team of assistants I assembled used the systems I created to work from home on weeknights and weekends even though personnel on other projects at NRI only worked from 9 to 5. As for my ability to facilitate the production of scientific manuscripts, this was largely driven by Key #1. Although Flanders sought my counsel on the development of joint publications, he very rarely followed the advice I gave for fear that it might upset other researchers at NRI. As a result, the current project only produced four scientific publications whereas the previous project I managed had produced a dozen scientific publications in the same amount of time.

Page 6

What drives *the second outcome you have chosen for analysis*?

The lack of freedom I had to implement operational strategies was principally driven by Keys #1 and #3. If I had been a match with Flanders on the dominant value at NRI, then the procedures I proposed would have been approved with the same expediency he used when reviewing the plans suggested by other research managers he collaborated with. Along the same lines, if I had been able to bridge the gaps in our relationship early on then I probably would have been given greater support during the implementation of these strategies.

Keys #1 and #3 also affected the opportunities I was given to collaborate with and learn from experts in the field. On past projects, I had easily earned the trust of Jackson and was often sent to key meetings as his proxy. Unfortunately, my misfit with Flanders and the barriers in our relationship prevented me from doing the same on this project.

If applicable, include analysis of why sensible people do senseless things.

Despite our disagreements and differences of opinion, Flanders never acted senselessly. Like me, he viewed his work as a calling and felt that his view of the world was correct from both a practical and moral standpoint. Since I had the same conviction about my own beliefs, the slight misfit between us on the dominant value at NRI became a recurring point of contention. Over time, it became clear that the best course of action was for me to make a lateral move within the organization. Besides Jackson, there were other researchers at NRI who shared my views and who would perceive my recommendations as both valuable and sensible.

Page 7

Assume that your knowledge of each of Keys #1 to #4 per your analysis above is given a score of 25. What is your score for your knowledge of Keys #1 to #4 *before* you accepted this job?

(a) **SCORE OUT OF 25 FOR: KEY 1 = 10; KEY 2 = 20; KEY 3 = 5; KEY 4 = 7.**

(b) **KEY #5: What did you miss when you were being recruited for this job?**

While being recruited for this job I failed to adequately analyze the hurdles I would have to overcome *(Question 8)*, the kind of person that was most respected *(Question 2)*, and my own attitudes toward my prospective boss *(Question 14)*. Had I taken the time to address these questions, I might have detected the resource challenges I would confront, the reasons Flanders was so well-respected, and the disagreements I would have about how to best manage personnel.

(c) **KEY #6: Were there any traps when you were being recruited for this job?**

When I was first considering the position, I was somewhat seduced by the organization. For instance, NRI offered me a prestigious title and a 20-percent salary increase if I managed Flanders' project. Since I had previously enjoyed working with Jackson, NRI was also an implicit favorite.

(d) **What should you have done differently when you were being recruited for this job?**

In retrospect, I should have taken more time to consider the impact that Flanders' values would have on the outcomes I was striving for. I also should have given less weight to the salary and title that was being offered to me by NRI.

Page 8

The lessons you have learned from this self-reflection analysis.

Prior to this analysis, I strived to maintain equal relations with all researchers at NRI. From a career perspective, this was a questionable decision. By failing to identify the key players whom my job performance relied upon, such as Flanders, I did not give these relationships the time and attention they deserved. If I were to repeat the same experience, I would make a concentrated effort to address the gaps in my relationship with Flanders beginning in early 2012.

Based on the analysis, it has also become apparent that I did not properly evaluate subtle cues exhibited by Flanders that expressed his opinion of our relationship. After re-reading all of my performance reviews, I realized that Flanders typically referred to me as a "great resource" and a "tremendous asset." However, he never described me as a trusted colleague. Another key indicator occurred in 2012. At that time, a series of office relocations were instituted. At the end of this period, I should have taken note of the fact that another research manager was positioned next to Flanders whereas as I was positioned close to Jackson.

A final lesson learned was the extent to which a misfit with the culture of an organization can affect one's career. In mid-2013, it was announced that Jackson would be stepping down as the director of the institute. This was due in large part to clashes he had with other researchers. In his place, Flanders was appointed as one of two co-directors. A few months later, I was privately approached by another researcher, Dr. Fielding, to take on a new project. I eagerly accepted even though this project was smaller than Flanders'. The deciding factor in this case was that I knew Dr. Fielding shared my values and would provide the freedom and career opportunities I desired.

APPENDIX 2

Harvard Cases That Can Be Used With This Book

Here is a brief description of select cases that I use with this book in my MBA and executive courses. All these cases are available from Harvard Business School Publishing at the URL, http://www.hbsp.harvard.edu/hbsp/index.jsp?_requestid=50091. Teaching notes are *not* available for these cases.

Part I: Strive to Create a Positive Impact for Your Organization and Yourself

Part I is assigned for pre-reading prior to the start of the course.

Part II: Determine Your "Values Gap" and Your "Skills, Effort, and Support Gap" *Before* Accepting a New Job

Case 1: Mike Miller (A) [HBS Case #482-061]

This is a good opening case because it shocks the students and gets them engaged in the course right away. As someone in class will eventually point out during the discussion of this case, Mike is so much like them and he runs into a mountain of trouble. Message: This can easily happen to you.

In Mike Miller (B), handed out after discussion of the (A) case, Mike is a good role model for MBA students—he takes responsibility for his mistakes, learns from them, and goes on to success in his next job.

Case 2: Kirk Stone (A) [HBS Case #482-067]

This is a good case to deliver a second shock, or to introduce students to the special challenges of joining a family-owned business.

Like Mike, Kirk does a poor job of understanding the company prior to accepting their job offer. Unlike Mike, Kirk is able to adapt and respond much better than Mike. Message: If you happen to be a *less* flexible person (that is, if you are more like Mike than Kirk), you need to *better* understand the job and the organization prior to accepting their offer.

Kirk Stone (B) provides additional data on the questions raised in the (A) case. Kirk is convinced his boss is behaving in an unethical manner, but a fair-minded assessment of the facts in the (B) case may lead some students to doubt this.

Message: When you encounter what you perceive to be unethical behavior, check the facts and seek the perspective of respected others before jumping to conclusions.

Case 3: Neill Hance [HBS Case #483-086]

This case provides a contrast to Mike Miller and Kirk Stone because Neill does better in understanding a difficult job and organizational situation prior to accepting their offer.

Neill runs into trouble at the end of the case because of difficulties with a key player, and this provides an opportunity to discuss the importance of maintaining good relationships and credibility with the key players (Keys #3 and #4).

Part III: Talk Less and Listen More for Effective Onboarding

Case 4: Eric Weiss [HBS Case #482-059]

Eric does not contribute anything to the organization he joins. If students dismiss him as weak, I ask how *they* would have handled the situation in Eric's place. This forces students to make sense of what seems senseless behavior, and reveals the agendas of the key players in the organization—and their expectations of Eric—which he misses completely.

Message: When you encounter strange or senseless behavior in an organization, ask yourself, "What is it that *I* don't understand that would make the senseless seem perfectly sensible?"

Case 5: Jody McVay [HBS Case #482-063]

Like Kirk Stone, Jody does not understand the organization well prior to entry but is flexible and responds to the situation creatively after joining in order to survive and succeed.

Part IV: Continue to Deliver Results and Make Other Contributions

Case 6: Dan Stewart (A) [HBS Case #482-087]

Dan Stewart is highly successful in several jobs in his company over 10 years but he does not realize how much his organization has changed until, one day, his subordinate who is on warning for poor performance is given a double promotion and becomes his boss!

Message: Seasoned executives—and not just newly minted MBAs—are susceptible to such shocks, and these are best viewed as invitations to understand the agendas of the key players and the organization's culture. The (B), (C), and (D) cases in this series reveal the specific challenges Dan faces as his career progresses.

Case 7: Jeff Bradley (A) [HBS Case #484-066]

Jeff, a new MBA, does a good job of understanding the organization before accepting their offer and then does a great job as a newcomer in a hostile work environment. He is a good role model for MBA students.

The (B) case describes Jeff's excellent contributions as a manager and as a leader.

Case 8: Buddy March [HBS Case #407-128]

As general manager of a division within a large corporation, Buddy has developed sufficient credibility to persist with a new venture that his boss opposes. This is a good case to discuss the challenges of contributing as an entrepreneur in a large organization.

Case 9: Mat MacGregor (A) [HBS Case #483-098]

Mat is the program manager for another venture championed by Buddy March, but this one is in trouble in part because Mat is not a good manager, nor a good leader, nor an entrepreneur. Why then was he appointed as program manager for this venture? Because no one else wanted the job and Mat could not say no to Buddy!

Message: Learn to say "no" when the mission is impossible for you. Mat, for example, discovered that he did not have the personality or the skill to manage his conflict with a key player on Buddy's team (Key #9) and yet he could not say no to this assignment because of a sense of loyalty to his boss and the chance to become the youngest general manager ever in his company.

Case 10: Mike Walker [HBS Case #484-061]

The case describes Mike's development from an introverted engineer to a superb manager, leader, and entrepreneur over a period of 22 years.

I have used this case to wrap up the course, or as a final exam for the course.

Notes

Preface

1. Lee (1966) used the term "self-reference criteria" to characterize our unconscious reference to our own cultural values, which can mislead us when
we deal with people from other cultures. Hofstede examined cross-cultural
differences on dimensions such as power distance, individualism versus col-
lectivism, and uncertainty avoidance (1980a), and explored the extent to
which American theories apply abroad (1980b). A classic textbook on the
subject by Adler and Gundersen (2008) examines national culture, workplace behavior across cultures, and other cross-cultural issues.

Introduction

1. One of the most complete and best-known career guides is *What Color Is
Your Parachute?* by Bolles (2008), first published in 1970 and updated an-
nually. Other sources are the collections of *Harvard Business Review* articles
on *Managing Your Career* (2002) and on *Managing Yourself* (2005). If you
are a mid-career professional who is questioning your career path after having made a long-term investment of time, energy, and education in that
path, the study by Ibarra (2004) provides insight into the process of career
transition, and offers nine unconventional strategies for reinventing your
career. If you feel that you have hit a dead end in your job or career or life,
see Butler (2007) for ways to move on by moving into and through whatever has you stuck. Also see Heslin (2005) and Schein (1996). As Greenhaus
and Callanan (1994, pp. 4–7) point out, a wide range of topics are included
within "career management."

2. This book belongs to the genre that looks at career management as an evolving sequence of a person's work experiences over time, including work-
related attitudes and behaviors. This is in line with Greenberg and Baron
(2008, p. 673): "Formally, a career can be defined as the evolving sequence
of work experiences over time."

3. The questions you should ask according to Drucker (2005): "What
should my contribution be? . . . What does the situation require? Given
my strengths, my way of performing, and my values, how can I make the

greatest contribution to what needs to be done? And finally, What results have to be achieved to make a difference?" (p. 106).

4. Greenberg and Baron (2008, p. 433) define organizational citizenship behavior (OCB) as "an informal form of behavior in which people go beyond what is formally expected of them to contribute to the well-being of the organization and those in it." OCB directed at an individual (e.g., assisting a coworker) is referred to as OCB-I and OCB of which the organization is the beneficiary is called OCB-O (e.g., offering ideas to improve the functioning of the organization). Five major categories of OCB are altruism (e.g., volunteering); conscientiousness (e.g., coming to work early if needed); civic virtue (e.g., attending voluntary meetings and functions); sportsmanship (e.g., making do without complaints); and courtesy (e.g., "turning the other cheek" to avoid problems). Also see Motowidlo and Van Scotter (1994); Organ and Lingl (1995); and Van Dyne and Pierce (2004).

5. See Odiorne (1974) for the activity trap. In *The Effective Executive*, his timeless classic first published in 1967, Drucker (2006) emphasizes the importance of contributing results, not activities, and indicates three broad areas of contribution for all executives: direct results, building of values and their affirmation, and building and developing people for tomorrow (pp. 52–55).

6. Martin (2007) shows the value of integrative thinking, the discipline of simultaneously considering opposing ideas to arrive at the creative synthesis that is better than either one of the alternatives. Thus, rather than thinking about what is best for the organization *versus* what is best for you, it is more challenging and potentially more rewarding to think about solutions that are superior for *both* the organization and for you. The benefits of combining opposites are also referred to in common parlance as "and" thinking, in contrast to "either or" thinking.

   DuBrin (2008) suggests that career and personal success are related, and that individuals can become more effective in both their careers and personal lives through improving their human relations skills.

7. If your contributions to the organization are intrinsically rewarding, this will have a positive impact on both your job satisfaction (how you *think* about your job) and also your happiness at work (how you *feel* about your job).

8. Mihaly Csikszentmihalyi (personal communication, April 4, 2006).

9. As *The Economist* (August 14, 2004, p. 69) puts it in reviewing the book *The Company of Strangers* by the economist Paul Seabright, "Our everyday life . . . is so much at odds with what would have seemed, as recently as 10,000 years ago, our evolutionary destiny. It is only then that one 'of the most aggressive and elusive bandit species in the entire animal kingdom' decided to settle down. In no more than a blink of an eye, in evolutionary time, these

suspicious and untrusting creatures, these 'shy, murderous apes,' developed co-operative networks of staggering scope and complexity—networks that rely on trust among strangers."

10. As Drucker (2005) puts it, "Very few people work by themselves and achieve results by themselves—a few great artists, a few great scientists, a few great athletes. Most people work with others and are effective with other people. That is true whether you are members of an organization or independently employed. Managing yourself requires taking responsibility for relationships" (p. 107).

11. Personal communication from my colleague Dick Ellsworth about how some of his students lost their ideals over the years as they pursued career success, and the importance of personal courage to avoid this danger.

Key #1

1. In their meta-analysis of the literature on a person's fit with his or her work environment (PE fit), Kristof-Brown, Zimmerman, and Johnson (2005, p. 325) recommend that, rather than ask for a global assessment of fit ("How well do you fit?"), it is more useful to consider at least four different types of fit: person's fit with the organization (PO fit), with the job (PJ fit), with one's superior (PS fit), and with one's group (PG fit). In this book, PJ fit is addressed in "Key #2: Your Fit With the Job", and PO, PS, and PG fits are covered in Key #1.

Fit is *complementary* when the characteristics of the individual fill a gap in the current environment, or vice versa. There are two types of complementary fit: (1) Demand–Abilities fit (DA fit)—does the individual have the abilities and skills required to meet the demands of the job—that is, the job challenges? DA fit is covered in Key #2. (2) Needs–Supplies fit (NS fit)—are the individual's needs met by the environmental supplies—in other words, does the organization satisfy the needs of the individual? (p. 288). NS fit is covered in Keys #1 and #2.

Fit is *supplementary* when the individual and the environment are similar. For example, do the individual and the organization have similar values? This is covered in Key #1. Research suggests that people have a fundamental need for consensual validation of their perspectives, which can be met by interacting with others with similar perspectives. So the fundamental mechanism of supplementary fit is also need fulfillment (Kristof-Brown, Zimmerman, & Johnson, 2005, p. 288). Also see Cable and Edwards (2004); Livingstone, Nelson, and Barr (1997); Montgomery (1996); Schneider (2001); Shaw and Gupta (2004); and Verquer, Beehr, and Wagner (2003).

2. These definitions follow Rokeach (1968) and Bem (1970).

3. Wilson (2002). *Blink* by Gladwell (2005) is a popular introduction to the powers of the unconscious mind.

4. Wilson (2002, p. 204). Also see the distinction between espoused values and values in use (Argyris & Schon, 1974).

5. McMurry (1963).

6. Spranger (1928) does not imply that a person belongs exclusively to one or another of the six basic types. Rather, his descriptions are entirely in terms of ideal types. The test developed to measure the relative strength of these values for an individual is Allport, Vernon, and Lindzey (1970). The test was originally developed by Allport and Vernon in 1931, and the revised version was first published by Allport, Vernon, and Lindzey in 1951. Guth and Tagiuri (1965) report results obtained for senior executives on the Spranger value classification scheme using the Allport, Vernon, and Lindzey test. The article also contains an excellent discussion of the importance of values for managers. Also see Kluckhohn (1951).

7. Sathe (1985) and Schein (1985).

8. Drucker (1994); Schein (1983, 1985); and Chao and Moon (2005).

9. The Attraction–Selection–Attrition (ASA) framework (Schneider, 1987) makes clear how the organization's culture is reinforced and sustained as people who share similar beliefs and values are attracted to the organization and join it, how the organization selects those who fit the culture, and how those who do not fit leave. Also see Schneider, Goldstein, and Smith (1995).

10. Harrison (1972). Missing in this scheme is the fundamental question that Selznick (1957) raised about whether the members of the organization view it merely as a *tool* to accomplish a certain purpose (so that the organization may be disbanded once the purpose is accomplished) or as an entity that is infused with *values* (so that it is not just a means to an end but an end that is worth preserving and defending). This missing dimension, the purpose of the organization, is included in our analysis using the Culture Map (Figure 5). Thanks to my colleague Dick Ellsworth for pointing this out.

11. Handy (1978).

12. The "competing values" framework developed by Cameron and Quinn (1999) reveals the value conflicts experienced in the cultures of most organizations.

13. *Personality* is "the unique and relatively stable pattern of behavior, thoughts, and emotions shown by individuals" (Greenberg & Baron, 2008, p. 135). Research indicates that one or more personality traits (e.g., the Big 5—extraversion, emotional stability, conscientiousness, agreeableness, and openness to experience—and Core Self Evaluations) have a direct influence on job performance, and/or job satisfaction. For example, Hurtz and Donovan

(2000) looked at the validity of the Big 5 measures in predicting job performance, and Lounsbury, Moffitt, Gibson, Drost, and Stevens (2007) studied personality traits in relation to job and career satisfaction of information technology (IT) professionals and found that independent, introverted individuals were better suited to jobs and careers as IT professionals.

The evidence on dispositional theory suggests that job satisfaction is a characteristic of the individual that stays fairly stable across situations. In effect, happy people tend to be happy regardless of where they work and those who have a negative disposition tend to be negative in any situation. Staw and Ross (1985) examine the argument that job attitudes are consistent within individuals over time and across situations. Staw and Cohen-Charash (2005) propose a new dispositional model of job satisfaction and discuss how dispositional affect can influence workplace experience. Also see Barrick, Mount, and Judge (2001); Judge, Heller, and Mount (2002); and Staw (2004).

Nevertheless, as Judge and Kristof-Brown (2004, p. 88) point out, "Clearly, there are main effects of personality on practically any meaningful attitude or behavior . . . those of us interested in the role of personality in applied psychology have been remiss in ignoring the environment and the interaction between the person and the environment." While personality researchers have neglected the environment, those who have studied PE fit have tended to focus on attributes of P (person) such as beliefs, values, skills, and abilities, rather than personality dimensions such as the Big 5 commonly studied by personality researchers. In their meta-analysis, Kristof-Brown, Zimmerman, and Johnson (2005, p. 322) found few studies in the vast literature on PE fit that considered the effects of personality dimensions such as the Big 5.

Lacking sufficient evidence on how personality dimensions such as the Big 5 *interact* with dimensions of the environment to influence behavior, I chose in this book to focus on the dimensions of P (beliefs, values, abilities, and skills) for which there is abundant research evidence.

14. A classic work on group norms is Sherif (1936).

15. One approach is for the individual to accept only the most central organizational beliefs and values. Such "creative individualism," as Schein (1968, pp. 3–10) calls it, may ultimately be in the best interest of the individual and the organization. Also see Freedman and Doob (1968); and Kiesler and Kiesler (1969).

Key #2

1. See Csikszentmihalyi (1990, 2003).

2. Called the Experience Method of Sampling (EMS), the researchers found that a person's happiness score varied considerably during the course of a

day, but the average daily EMS score (i.e., a person's average level of happiness during a day) tended to remain constant from one day to the next. Job satisfaction scores typically show little variation within a single day or from one day to the next (Mihaly Csikszentmihalyi, personal communication, April 24, 2006).

3. See Locke (2004). The importance of clear goals and expectations is covered in Key #3 and getting feedback to monitor how you are doing is discussed in Key #8.

4. See Carr (2004), Myers (1992), and Seligman (2002).

5. In Csikszentmihalyi (2003, p. 67), "Boredom" appears in the right corner; more recent work places "boredom" closer to "apathy," with the right corner now labeled "relaxation" (Mihaly Csikszentmihalyi, personal communication, April 24, 2006).

6. This result is consistent with PE fit research (Kristof-Brown, Zimmerman, & Johnson, 2005, p. 310) as follows: The traditional way of measuring fit by comparing P and E scores on profiles such as the Organizational Culture Profile (OCP) does not make a distinction between fit at lower or higher levels of P and E. For example, the results when P and E both equal 1 ($P - E = 1 - 1 = 0$) are no different than when P and E both equal 9 ($P - E = 9 - 9 = 0$); in both cases the difference is 0, a perfect fit. But research using polynomial regression methodology by Edwards (1993, 1996) revealed that fit at high levels of P and E was associated with better results than fit at low levels of P and E, which is exactly what Csikszentmihalyi and his colleagues have found with the EMS methodology (Figure 7). Low skills (P) and low challenges (E) does not produce flow, it produces apathy. High skills (P) and high challenges (E) produces flow. See O'Reilly, Chatman, and Caldwell (1991) for OCP.

7. I wish to thank Madhu Karve for a conversation that helped me to clarify the argument in this section.

8. In contrast, the relationship between job satisfaction and job performance has been studied extensively and the results are inconclusive. Judge, Thoresen, Bono, and Patton (2001) tested seven models of the relationship between job satisfaction and job performance, and reported inconsistent results from two meta-analyses. A third meta-analysis using 312 different samples and a combined sample size of 54,417 respondents found a mean true correlation of 0.30 between job satisfaction and job performance.

9. Others have reported some evidence of better results when your skills exceed the challenges than when your skills are equal to the challenges. For example, the latest research by Csikszentmihalyi and his colleagues indicates that the well-documented finding that happiness peaks when challenges and skills are in balance is only obtained for people engaged in a

task *primarily for its intrinsic rewards.* For those who are engaged in a task *primarily for its extrinsic rewards* (such as pay, perks, etc.), happiness peaks when skills *exceed* job challenges, perhaps because people want to be sure to receive the extrinsic reward they are seeking (Mihaly Csikszentmihalyi, personal communication, April 24, 2006).

As another example, the polynomial regression methodology of Edwards (1993, 1996) also revealed that, for Needs–Supplies (NS) fit, the condition of supplies greater than needs was associated with better results. If these results hold for the analogous conditions of abilities (skills) in excess of demands (challenge), they would be consistent with the latest findings from Csikszentmihalyi and his colleagues, and with what I am proposing here.

10. Gardner (2006).

11. Menkes (2005).

12. Goleman (1995, 1998).

13. Burud and Tumolo (2004, Chapter 4). Individuals who place greater importance on marriage and family do *not* pay a price for that priority in subsequent labor market success, according to research by Cappelli, Constantine, and Chad-wick (2000).

14. Herzberg, Mausner, and Synderman (1959). The literature on compliance versus commitment (Kelman, 1958) closely parallels this work, with extrinsic motivation producing compliance and intrinsic motivation producing commitment. The acid test of intrinsic motivation is that the work you are doing is itself rewarding—no other inducement external to the work itself is necessary for you to do it. Also see Christen, Iyer, and Soberman (2006).

15. Bellah, Madsen, Sullivan, Swidler, and Tipton (2008).

16. Derived from Ellsworth (2002).

17. In the original model proposed by Herzberg, Mausner, and Synderman (1959), intrinsic motivation for working included opportunities for advancement, achievement, and recognition, but more recent work views these as a combination of extrinsic and intrinsic motivation.

18. Wrzesniewski (2003, p. 301).

19. One of the eight career anchors observed by Schein (1996) is "service/dedication to a cause," and he states, "The number of people showing up with this anchor is increasing. More and more young people, as well as mid-life career occupants, report that they are feeling the need not only to maintain an adequate income, but to do something meaningful in a larger context" (p. 85).

20. Sathe and Tyabji (2007, p. 13) offer the following example: "Transcendence is more than enlightened self-interest, which meets the interests of others in a way that is consistent with self-interest. For example, while mentoring helps others, it also satisfies the mentor's need to give something back to

the next generation. To understand how transcendence goes beyond this, consider this example from everyday life given by the philosopher Alfred Schopenhauer.

A bystander, without thinking, puts his own life at risk by leaping to save a total stranger who is about to fall off a cliff. How can one explain this selfless behavior? Schopenhauer views it as an example of transcendence; in that moment, the other's interest becomes one's own interest. If transcendence is possible with a total stranger, it is certainly possible with one's associates at work."

21. Maslow (1943) and McClelland (1961).

22. Maslow (1971, p. 42).

23. Maslow, Stephens, and Heil (1998); and Richard Ellsworth (personal communication, November 4, 2005).

24. Csikszentmihalyi (1990, pp. 92, 209).

25. As Csikszentmihalyi (1990, pp. 216–217) points out, how we use our limited psychic energy is important to our well-being and personal growth. When focused on causes outside of ourselves that we deeply care about, we achieve harmony and become more complex and fully developed human beings. Also see Ellsworth (2002, pp. 80–82). Thus, it is possible to avoid the increasingly common condition called "attention deficit trait," which is turning steady executives into frenzied underachievers (see Hallowell, 2005).

26. Wrzesniewski, McCauley, Rozin, and Schwartz (1997); and A. Wrzesniewski (personal communication, March 6, 2007). Hall and Chandler (2005) explore the relationship between subjective and objective careers and specifically examine an individual's sense of a career as a calling.

27. Work design (Hackman & Oldham, 1980; Morgeson, Delaney-Klinger, & Hemingway, 2005) can influence job enlargement and job enrichment, but some people may view the work as a job while others may view it as a calling. Wrzesniewski (2003, p. 303) provides a compelling illustration of a cleaner, Maria, who views her work as a calling whereas others view it as just a job.

28. Wrzesniewski (2003, p. 305). The new reality, according to Burud and Tumolo (2004), is that "dual-focus" workers outnumber by three to one (p. 40) workers who have a partner at home to provide support, and these dual-focus workers find a singular focus on work undesirable and often impossible (p. 52). A question for future research is whether there are dual-focus workers for whom work is a calling and, if so, how they manage work–life balance.

29. Wrzesniewski (2003, p. 302).

30. Wrzesniewski and Dutton (2001); and Wrzesniewski (2003, pp. 300–304).

31. Based on research in progress.

32. There is plenty of evidence that too many resources are as bad as too few. The danger of too few resources is obvious; with too many resources, the danger is of a proliferation of projects that are not clearly thought through, a lack of urgency and focus, and complacency (Sathe, 2003, Chapter 16). The classic work of Stewart (1982) shows that a manager must make wise choices given the demands and the constraints he or she faces in light of the resources available.

33. See Key #10, section on "Becoming a Manager," for more on high-performance work practices (HPWPs).

34. "General Electric Alumni Find It Harder to Shine," *The Wall Street Journal*, May 15, 2003, p. A1.

35. Support from colleagues, and from the organization at large, has both a task and an emotional dimension. See Eisenberger, Huntington, Hutchison, and Sowa (1986) for early work on perceived organizational support. Also see Rhoads and Eisenberger (2002); Rhoads, Eisenberger, and Armeli (2001); Ducharme and Martin (2000); and Erdogan and Enders (2007). Research also indicates the importance of having friends in the workplace (Yoneshige, 2005); having a best friend at work is associated with feeling happy at work. Gallup's survey of 12 questions (G12) to measure employee engagement has one item, "Do you have a best friend at work?" that is positively correlated with engagement. See Buckingham and Coffman (1999) for background on this research.

36. The importance of clear expectations is covered in Key #3 and the importance of early feedback is discussed in Key #8.

Key #3

1. Derived from Gabarro (1978) and Walton (1968). Group dynamics also come into play. For example, you may be forced to take sides, or be accepted into one group, which makes it more difficult for you to develop good relationships with people in a rival group. Thanks to Avinash Nene for pointing this out.

2. Schein (1995) provides a strategic job and role planning guide for thinking about how your job relates to other people's expectations, who the key stakeholders are for your job, what the key stakeholder expectations are, the changes in these expectations over time, and the implications for you.

3. Among the three sets of cognitive skills identified by Menkes (2005) is the ability to recognize underlying agendas.

4. Kotter and Lawrence (1974); Stewart (1979); and Argyris (1982). Our new understanding of how the mind works explains why this is so common—our

conscious mind has no direct access to our unconscious agendas, which are best discovered by observing how we *behave* rather than what we *say* (Wilson, 2002, p. 35, Chapter 9).

5. The bases of trust that rest on competence are also bases of power (expertise, broadly defined), but they are included here because Gabarro (1978) indicates that, in the business setting at least, managers think of both bases of character and competence when they speak of trust. See Aryee, Budhwar, and Chen (2002) for a discussion of trust as a mediator of the relationship between organizational justice and work outcomes. Also see Deutsch (1962); Ferrin and Dirks (2003); and Lewicki, McAllister, and Bies (1998) for understanding trust and distrust within relationships; and a special topic forum on trust in and between organizations in the July 1998 issue of *The Academy of Management Review*. For the importance of trust in human development, see "The Story of Man," *The Economist*, December 25, 2005, p. 11.

6. Argyris (1982).

7. The list is based on the works of Gabarro (1979) as well as Kotter (1977). Also see Bachrach and Baratz (1962); Bacharach and Lawler (1980); Cialdini (1993); and Pfeffer (1981).

8. The classic experiments of Milgram (1963, 1965) and Zimbardo (1971) leave no doubt that, under coercive conditions, people will obey authority figures. Fortunately, the modern workplace does not conform very well to these conditions, certainly in the developed economies and increasingly in the developing world, but it is important to remember how easily these conditions can be created.

9. Wall (2000) provides 30 exercises to sharpen skills and become more aware of what you can do to make relationships work.

Key #4

1. Asher points out that "doing your job is not enough to get promoted. . . . The question is: do you want to manage your career or just experience it?" (2007, p. vi). The book offers school-of-hard-knocks strategies for positioning oneself for promotion, such as getting noticed, making the boss look good, and finding guardian angels and benefactors.

2. See Aronson (1976, p. 175).

3. Kanter (1977). See Chapter 8 of her book, "Numbers: Minorities and Majorities."

4. You may also be stereotyped because you are perceived as part of another group in the organization.

5. Kanter (1977, pp. 210–211) uses the term "assimilation" for "stereotyping."

6. This response is not mentioned by Kanter (1977); it is a token strategy that was observed in the cases that I have developed for the course on which this book is based.

7. Some prejudice may be a reflection of the individual's own insecurities. The highly prejudiced individual may deny or repress his or her own weaknesses by projecting them onto the objects of the prejudice. See Bem (1970, Chapter 3).

8. Sutton (2007) calls such people "assholes." You may be offended by his use of this term or you may feel that it is a provocative reminder of the harm that such people inflict on others. Either way, in my view, Sutton's valuable book does not pay sufficient attention to the danger that we may stereotype someone as an "asshole" just because we don't like that person. The stereotype may create a self-fulfilling prophecy rather than an opening for change. So it is better to talk about asshole *behavior*. Sutton offers two tests for asshole identification: (1) a person who makes others feel oppressed, humiliated, de-energized, or belittled, and (2) a person who aims his or her venom at people who are *less powerful* rather than at people who are more powerful (p. 9). People who are behaving like assholes and jerks may be tolerated because they are seen as powerful or indispensable by their targets or others.

Lubit (2002) defines and describes "destructively narcissistic (DN) managers and leaders"—why they are able to survive and prosper in some organizations despite their destructive behavior, how people can recognize DN managers more quickly, how to design organizations to decrease the prevalence of DN managers, and how to deal with them. "Moving to another position with the company in order to avoid the DN manager is generally the best long-term strategy" (2002, p. 137).

9. I am indebted to my faculty colleague, attorney Rafael Chodos, for this personal communication regarding legal remedies that may or may not be available in U.S. courts, particularly in California: "Having a 'jerk' in the workplace whom the higher-ups refuse to discipline may make the work environment feel hostile but by itself it does *not* give rise to a remedy under the law. The missing ingredient is the violation of some statute: usually some provision of the Fair Employment and Housing Act (Government Code Sec. 12900-12996), which prohibits discrimination based on age, gender, or race; or the Whistleblower Protection Act (Government Code Sec. 8547.3), which prohibits retaliating against an employee for reporting bad conduct—any bad conduct (cheating the government on pricing issues, as well as violations of workplace safety laws and discrimination laws). When the 'jerk' is in effect engaging in sexual harassment, or age discrimination, or unlawful retaliation, then the refusal of the higher-ups to intervene may be actionable."

Rafael Chodos continues (personal communication): "In *Meritor Savings v. Vinson* (1986) 477 US 57, the Supreme Court distinguished two different kinds of sexual harassment: in one type of case, economic benefits are conditioned on sexual favors, as when a supervisor tells an employee, 'Sleep with me and I will recommend you for a raise' or 'Unless you sleep with me, I will have you demoted.' This is called 'quid pro quo' harassment. But the other kind is called 'hostile work environment': the work environment is sexually discriminatory but there is no focused, quid pro quo harassment. The hostile environment is created by the fellow workers, who are the 'jerks' and 'assholes' (to use Sutton's term), and the employer tolerates their behavior. It is against the law to create or tolerate a sexually discriminatory hostile work environment, and if such an environment can be shown, the employee may have a remedy. The notion arises also in cases where an employee becomes a whistleblower and the employer, too sophisticated to fire that employee or demote him or her, still retaliates by creating a hostile work environment for him or her. The employee might be reassigned to a different department, have his or her working conditions altered in a thousand ways—and sometimes the courts find that all that adds up to a form of retaliation, which is prohibited by the Whistleblower Protection Act."

Rafael Chodos concludes (personal communication): "So while the courts, particularly in California, are receptive to claims that the work environment is hostile, the claims cannot be brought simply because one's coworkers are jerks. The hostility has to consist of discrimination OR it has to be a form of retaliation. An employee who tells his superiors, 'my coworkers are jerks and I need you to do something about it,' and gets no reaction at all and then sues over it—such an employee would lose, I think. A point to bear in mind is that the courts probably can't, and shouldn't, stick their collective nose into every social interaction in the workplace. In the dance of life we step on each other's toes, and if every misstep gave rise to a potential lawsuit, we'd never be able to enjoy the music. The mere fact that someone is a jerk and behaves badly can't by itself give rise to a legal remedy: there has to be some lofty principle at stake, which the legislature, in its infinite wisdom, has seen fit to embody in legal rules (e.g., prohibitions against certain kinds of discrimination)." In connection with the dance of life, see Wall (2000).

For reference, see Rafael Chodos, *The Law of Fiduciary Duties, With Citations to the California Authorities* (2001), a comprehensive, authoritative treatise and practice aid, tracing the law of fiduciary duties through its historical layers, right through current California cases. Available from Blackthorne Legal Press, Malibu, California, in both hardcover (1,650 pages) and CD-ROM formats. Also on Amazon.com.

10. As my student Xueyun Guan points out, "there is a strong connection between danger and opportunity in the Chinese character for 'crisis' (危机). Taken separately, the character (危) means danger, and the other character (机) means opportunity."

Part II

1. There is always the danger that one is simply rationalizing past actions, a possibility that must be discounted for and guarded against.

Key #5

1. The book by Clawson, Kotter, Faux, and McArthur (1992) is a valuable resource for self-assessment and career development. McCall (1998, Appendix) provides guidance for taking charge of your own development.

2. Wanous (1980) provides a summary discussion of the assessment center approach and its limitations (pp. 143–159).

3. In addition to technical problems having to do with reliability (does the test produce consistent results?) and validity (does the test measure what it is supposed to measure?), the more basic problem is that such tests only reveal what one *thinks* one believes, values, does, or would do. What one espouses about these and other matters may or may not be closely related to one's actual position as revealed by the choices one in fact makes and the way in which one actually behaves. Further, one may not even be conscious of such discrepancies between espoused and actual values, as pointed out by Argyris and Schon (1974) and confirmed by what we now know about the unconscious mind (Wilson, 2002).

4. Schein (2006) offers a self-assessment guide to help you discover your *career anchor*, which is "that combination of perceived areas of competence, motives and values that *you discover you would not give up* if you faced a career decision that might not allow you to fulfill it. It represents your real self. Without knowledge of your anchor, outside incentives might tempt you into situations or jobs that subsequently are not satisfactory because you feel that 'this is not really me.' The questionnaire in this booklet is intended to help you figure out who you really are" (pp. v–vii). The survey Strengthfinder 2.0 is designed to give you insight into your top five themes of talent: "Our studies indicate that people who *do* have the opportunity to focus on their strengths every day are *six times as likely to be engaged in their jobs*" (Rath, 2007, p. iii; emphasis original). Another survey, focusing on your instinctive talents, is available from Kolbe (1990–1997).

5. Stewart (1979, p. 35).

6. Full of vivid real-life examples, McCall (1998) shows why the real leaders of the future are those who have the ability to learn from their experiences and remain open to continuous learning. See, in particular, Chapter 3. The book by Wademan (2004) is a collection of 15 life stories from faculty members at Harvard Business School that provide inspiration and direction for anyone seeking to create not just a good career but a good life. One of the three important cognitive skills identified by Menkes (2005) is the ability to identify one's own mistakes, encourage and seek out constructive criticism, and adjust one's own behavior.

7. de Charms (1968), and Rotter (1966).

8. Finkelstein (2003) studied 51 companies and discovered that precipitous business failures are caused by four destructive patterns: (1) flawed executive mind-sets that throw off a company's perception of reality, (2) delusional attitudes that keep this inaccurate reality in place, (3) breakdowns in communication, and (4) leadership that keeps the company from correcting its course. As Pfeffer and Sutton (2006) point out, "power, prestige, and performance make you stubborn, stupid, and resistant to change" (p. 225).

9. Adams (2004) argues that the kind of questions you ask yourself can profoundly affect your self-esteem, relationships, and career.

10. Constructive introspection is particularly difficult in connection with experiences that are personally threatening or painful because one's defense mechanisms are geared to deal with these situations realistically and rationally only to the extent possible, and illogically and irrationally to the extent necessary (see Rokeach, 1968, pp. 9, 164, 182). Pain, like body fever, should be viewed as a symptom that indicates something is wrong and that additional investigation is needed. With the frame of mind that says, "pain is my friend, pain is invitation to learning," constructive introspection becomes possible. Zaleznik (1967) argues that with such introspection it is possible for one's disappointments to become occasions for accelerated personal growth and mark the commencement of truly outstanding performance.

11. This conclusion is based on her study of 39 people who changed careers (Ibarra, 2004, p. 161).

12. The "mind–body" problem of Descartes was a false dichotomy because it not only endowed the mind with a special status that was unrelated to the physical laws but also restricted the mind to consciousness, thus eliminating the possibility of unconscious thought (Wilson, 2002, p. 9; Damasio, 1994).

13. Wilson (2002, p. 204).

14. The best diagnostic question, according to Pfeffer and Sutton (2006, p. 232), is "what happens when people fail?" The best organizations "forgive and remember" so as to learn from their failures.

15. The book by Pondy, Frost, Morgan, and Dandridge (1983) contains several papers, particularly in Chapter 3, that explain how culture is propagated and transmitted via language, stories, folklore, sagas, myths, ceremonies, rituals, slogans, and other symbolic means.

16. This question is from Levinson (1972). Appendix A of Levinson's book (pp. 520–526) contains a comprehensive list of questions for use by consultants undertaking an organizational diagnosis. Because the skill, perspective, and relationship of a consultant with an organization are different than those of a person contemplating joining the organization, the latter cannot always ask questions like the former can. Levinson's list, therefore, should not be used by prospective employees for interviewing during recruiting without taking this underlying difference into account. The list does provide good food for thought, however.

17. This question is from Levinson (1972).

18. A discussion of the dynamics of stereotyping is included in Key #4.

19. If one has a frame of mind built on the assumption that one will invariably be stereotyped, one can always find the "facts" to support this, partly by behaving in a way that produces the facts one is looking for. Those who have experienced the trauma of severe stereotyping are understandably prone to do this, but that does not diminish its self-destructive potential.

20. Gabarro and Kotter (1980) present thoughtful suggestions for better managing your relationship with your boss. Ott, Blacksmith, and Royal (2007) report that when seeking employment, those being hired are much more attracted to the quality of a company's management than to potential perks.

21. This question looks at where attention is focused in the organization. As argued by Simon (1973, pp. 268–278), modern information processing systems feed today's organizations with an increasingly rich soup of information; in this environment, it is not information per se but attention that is the scarce resource. Much can be learned about the functioning of an organization by understanding how this critical resource is allocated.

22. The discussion of homosocial reproduction in the next chapter elaborates on this phenomenon.

Key #6

1. An excellent discussion relevant to the reading of people's use of time, space, things, body language, and words is contained in the first three chapters of Athos and Gabarro (1978).

2. Several authors have advocated *realistic recruitment* and *realistic job previews* for their salutary effects on employee turnover, satisfaction, and

effectiveness. The former attempts to provide the recruit with all pertinent information without distortion, the latter attempts to set employee expectations closer to reality, thereby "vaccinating" the individual against later disappointment and disillusionment. Much of the earlier work looks at the problem primarily from the organization's perspective. See Weitz (1956) and McGuire (1964). Later work includes the individual's perspective as well. See Buckley, Veres, Fedor, Wiese, and Carraher (1998); Schein (1978); Wanous (1980, 1989); and Wanous, Poland, Premack, and Davis (1992).

Barrick and Zimmerman (2005) examined clear-purpose retention scales and disguised-purpose retention scales to assess voluntary turnover. They found that regardless of which scale was used prehire attitudes and dispositions, along with behavioral intentions, predicted voluntary and organizationally avoidable turnover.

3. The book by Schein (1978) contains an excellent elaboration of these dynamics and dilemmas of the period prior to entry (see Chapter 7 of his book).

4. Lewicki (1981). Lewicki does not explicitly emphasize the organization's intent to conceal damaging information from the individual while attempting to attract him or her as the test of seduction. The position taken here is that, without such an explicit test, the term "organizational seduction" does not take on the tone of impropriety that usefully distinguishes it from other more common forms of enticement, such as those mentioned in the text under "Organizational Oversell."

5. Salancik (1977, pp. 62–80).

6. I am indebted to Jeffrey Pfeffer of Stanford University for suggesting this label, in lieu of "Homosexual Reproduction," which is the original phrase coined by Moore (1962); see Kanter (1977, p. 48).

7. Wanous (1980) reports research that indicates judgments of interviewers may be affected by the degree of similarity between interviewer and job candidate (p. 142). Sathe (1982) found evidence of "inbreeding"—companies whose CEO had a financial background has a significantly higher proportion of top executives also with financial backgrounds than did other companies. See Van Vianen (2000).

8. See Kanter (1977, pp. 48–54).

9. Based on a study of 96 active job seekers, Cable and Judge (1996) found that PO fit perceptions based on values congruence are related to job choice intentions and work attitudes. Demographic similarity did not predict job seekers' fit perceptions, so decisions made on the basis of surface similarities are more likely to be hiring mistakes.

10. Springbelt (1958, pp. 13–22).

11. Lawler and Rhode (1976). Page 1 and Chapter 6, in particular, contain good illustrations and a discussion of misuse of measurement systems.

12. Schein (1978, p. 85).

13. Soelberg (1967, pp. 19–29).

14. Cognitive dissonance theory predicts that an individual will gather information after the decision is made in order to justify it, to reduce postdecision "dissonance." See Festinger (1957).

15. O'Reilly and Caldwell (1981, pp. 597–616).

16. Wilson (2002, pp. 43–49, 125).

17. Wilson (2002, pp. 90–91). He includes evidence indicating that people whose conscious and nonconscious personalities were in sync showed greater emotional well-being.

18. Damasio (1994) demonstrates that emotions are not a luxury; they are essential to rational thinking and to normal social behavior: "emotions and feelings may not be intruders in the bastion of reason at all: they may be enmeshed in its networks, for worse *and* for better . . . emotions and feelings can cause havoc in the processes or reasoning under certain circumstances. . . . It is thus even more surprising and novel that the *absence* of emotion and feeling is no less damaging, no less capable of compromising the rationality that makes us distinctively human" (p. xvi; emphases original).

19. Janis (1972); and Janis and Wheeler (1978).

20. Your trusted friend should be someone who cares enough about you to tell you the truth, even if you do not appreciate it. As Aristotle said, friendship is central to human relationships, and he identified three very different types of friendship: Type 1—those based on transaction (I do something for you and you do something for me); Type 2—those based on pleasure (we enjoy each other's company); and Type 3—the rarest form, those based on seeking for the other what is best for the other. Your trusted friend should be Aristotle's Type 3 (Sathe and Tyabji, 2007, pp. 12–13).

Part III

1. Ball (2003) offers advice on making the transition from college to workplace by negotiating the challenges of entry-level jobs. Also see Holton and Naquin (2001); Kaye and Jordan-Evans (2003); and Usheroff (2004). Nelson (2001) contends that the key to helping the organization and achieving personal success is to fulfill what he terms "the ultimate expectation." This demands that individuals use their best judgment about what needs to be done and then do it, instead of waiting to be told what to do.

2. Newcomers just out of college are not the only ones who are vulnerable. The pages of the business press are full of CEOs and other senior executives who do not last long in their new jobs.

Key #7

1. Avery (1960); Van Maanen (1976, pp. 78–80, 117); Ashforth, Saks, and Lee (1998); Watkins reports that each year slightly fewer than a quarter of the managers in a typical *Fortune 500* company change jobs (2003, p. 7).

2. Van Maanen (1976, p. 78).

3. Watkins introduces the notion of "the breakeven point" as that point, typically 6 months after entering a new organization, at which the newcomer has contributed as much value to the organization as he or she has consumed from it (2003, p. 3).

4. Reported in "Starting a New Job? Don't Blow It" by Anne Fisher (*Fortune*, March 7, 2005, p. 48).

5. Louis (1980, pp. 226–251).

6. This staged conceptualization of the process of acquiring cultural knowledge is proposed by Siehl and Martin (1981).

7. This observation is from the cases developed for the course on which this book is based.

8. Anakwe and Greenhaus (1999) developed measures of socialization effectiveness (task mastery, work group functioning, knowledge and acceptance of the culture, personal learning, and role clarity) and found that experienced members of the organization were critical in fostering effective socialization.

9. See Harvard Business School (2004) and Stone (2007).

10. Thompson (2005) studied the relationship between proactive personality and job performance and suggested that proactive employees develop social networks that allow them to pursue high-level initiatives and thus gain performance benefits. Rollag, Parise, and Cross (2005) point out that the key to making employees productive quickly, known as "rapid on-boarding," is to help them immediately build an informational network with coworkers. Kim, Cable, and Kim (2005) found that a firm's socialization tactics and PO fit were facilitated or negated by several proactive behaviors that employees used to gain control over their environment. For example, employees who proactively developed strong relationships with their supervisors essentially replaced institutionalized socialization tactics. As Ibarra and Hunter (2007) point out, "Savvy managers reach out to kindred spirits outside their organizations to contribute and multiply their knowledge; the information they gain, in more cases than not, becomes the 'hook' for making internal connections" (p. 47).

11. Hughes (1958).

12. "Total institutions" have close to absolute control over their members; see Goffman (1961). In such institutions (e.g., mental hospitals, prisons, religious cults), newcomers are typically socialized by harsh methods and experience more intense shocks during the process. See Dornbush (1955, pp. 316–321).

13. Van Maanen (1984).
14. Schein (1978, p. 95).
15. Cases developed for the course on which this book is based bear this out.
16. Lyman and Scott (1970). From this perspective, socialization may be understood as equivalent to the coping strategies developed by stage neophytes, such as rehearsals when they follow the lines strictly.
17. Korman (1968).
18. Kotter (1982, p. 47).
19. Research indicates that meaningful and challenging first assignments are generally a very effective method of breaking in the newcomer. Such meaningful early testing can also pave the way for accelerated individual development and contribution to the organization. See Schein (1978).
20. Schein (1978, p. 106).
21. Gabarro (1979, 1987, 2007).
22. Successive gains in credibility appear to take place more slowly than successive losses. For example, 5 points may be lost the first time a critical incident is poorly managed by the newcomer, 15 points may be lost in the next one, 50 in the third, and so on.
23. One of the principles that Pfeffer and Sutton (2006) offer to implement evidence-based management is "See yourself and your organization as outsiders do" (p. 224).
24. Decisions should not be made on the basis of "sunk costs," of course, but rather on the basis of future streams of costs and benefits associated with various courses of action. The newcomer is at an advantage because one's organization-specific knowledge, skill, and status, which generally rise the longer one stays in an organization, would not be fully transportable if one were to leave.

Key #8

1. Wanberg and Kammeyer-Mueller (2000) found that two of the Big 5 personality variables, extraversion and openness to experience, were associated with higher levels of proactive socialization. Of the proactive behaviors studied, *feedback seeking* and *relationships building* were the most strongly related to outcomes such as social integration, role clarity, job satisfaction, intention to remain, and actual turnover.
2. Schein (1978, Chapter 9).
3. van Gennep (1960).
4. In a longitudinal study that began with 461 job seekers about 6 months prior to graduation, of whom 129 responded to a follow-up survey 6 months after graduation (and 33 percent of these 129 responded a year after that [pp. 10–11]), Cable and Parsons (2001, pp. 16–18) found that newcomers

were more likely to move toward their organization's values when they experienced sequential and fixed socialization (i.e., they received information concerning the sequence and timetable associated with career progression), and serial and investiture socialization (i.e., newcomers received positive social support from experienced organizational members).

5. Van Maanen (1976, p. 111).

6. As Wilson (2002, p. 212) points out: "If we want to become a better person, we should follow a 'do good, be good' strategy. By acting in ways that are helpful and caring toward others, we will come to view ourselves as more helpful and caring people."

7. Schein (1964) indicates that substantive individual change can occur in organizations within the context of "affective" relationships—that is, those characterized by personal rapport and positive feelings.

8. Schein (1968, p. 11).

9. Louis (1980, p. 231) points out that for a long time research on organizational socialization focused on the "joining-up" process and virtually ignored the "leave-taking" process. There are indications from related literature that the latter may significantly influence the former.

10. Schein (1978, Chapter 9).

Part IV

1. Zaleznik (2004); and Kotter (1990). My research in progress shows that there is considerable overlap between the *behaviors* associated with the role of manager, leader, and entrepreneur as defined in the literature on these roles.

Key #9

1. Badaracco (2002) describes and applauds "quiet leaders" who choose responsible, behind-the-scenes action to do the right thing. Reardon (2007) shows how to know the difference between political courage and political suicide.

2. Bem (1970, Chapter 5).

3. Sathe (1982).

4. See Pondy, Frost, Morgan, and Dandridge (1983).

5. *Argumentation: Understanding and Shaping Arguments* by Herrick (2004) is a highly accessible book on argumentation.

6. The idea that deviating from the prevailing culture drains one's credibility (i.e., uses up one's existing credit) goes all the way back to Hollander (1958, pp. 117–127).

7. Martin and Siehl (1983, pp. 52–64). "The Absorption of Protest" by Leeds (1964) is a classic.

8. Saturn Corporation cases from Harvard Business School Publishing. Saturn: A different kind of car company—Case #9-795-010; Saturn Corp. in 1996—Case #9-797-052; Saturn Corp. in 1998—Case #9-799-021.

9. *Organization and Environment: Managing Differentiation and Integration* by Lawrence and Lorsch (1967) is the original classic.

10. Avinash Nene (personal communication, October 27, 2007).

11. Several studies have highlighted the importance of constructive airing and resolution of conflict to enhance organizational effectiveness. See Lawrence and Lorsch (1967); and Janis (1972).

12. See Allen, Madison, Porter, Renwick, and Mayes (1979).

13. See O'Day (1974).

14. Avinash Nene (personal communication, October 27, 2007).

15. Walton (1969).

Key #10

1. People differ in terms of the life cycle stage of the business that they are better at handling. Some are better at handling the start-up and growth stages, when innovation and entrepreneurship are critical. Others are better at handling the maturity and decline stages, when asset management, including efficiency and cost reduction, and leadership are the keys to success. People begin to make contributions in management, leadership, or entrepreneurship because of differences in personal inclination and training, and differences in the circumstances they encounter in their early careers. As they acquire a reputation for success in one of these areas, they get called on to play to those strengths again, which builds their strengths in that area further (Sathe, 2003, pp. 96–97).

2. See Hill (2003, 2007).

3. The "better, faster, cheaper" mantra at the Jet Propulsion Laboratory (JPL) is a case in point (personal communication with several executive students from JPL).

4. Bossidy, Charan, Burck, and Smith (2002).

5. Ulrich, Kerr, and Ashkenas (2002).

6. Jack Welch video, Edward Jones investment seminar, © Edward Jones, 1999.

7. Charan, Drotter, and Noel (2001). The "turns" in Figure 12 are from Stephen Drotter's presentation in my class on April 17, 2004. Also see "GE's Talent Machine: The Making of a CEO," Harvard Business School Case #9-304-049, Rev. May 5, 2004.

8. Charan, Drotter, and Noel (2001).

9. From Stephen Drotter's presentation in my class on April 17, 2004. Also see "From Functional Manager to Business Leader: How Companies Can Help," in Ibarra and Hunter (2007, p. 46).

10. Fernandez-Araoz (2007, p. 4); emphasis original.

11. Smart and Smart (2005). Regarding retention, Mitchell, Holtom, Lee, Sablynski, and Erez (2001) defined people's "job embeddedness" as their (1) links to other people, teams, and groups; (2) perception of their fit with the job, organization, and community; and (3) what they say they would have to sacrifice if they left their jobs, and found that it predicted intention to leave and voluntary turnover (the converse of retention) over and above the traditional predictors such as job satisfaction and organizational commitment.

12. Smart and Smart (2005). What we know about improving customer retention may be usefully applied to increasing employee retention—by viewing employees as customers. For example, the research that led to the SERVQUAL method of comparing customer service quality performance with customer service quality needs (Parasuraman, Berry, & Zeithaml, 1991) found that *reliability* (the ability to perform the promised service dependably and accurately) was the most important factor affecting service quality. If employees are viewed as customers, what is the "service" that managers must perform for them with *reliability?* Focusing on this service will improve employee retention and satisfaction (Avinash Nene, personal communication, October 6, 2007).

13. See Huselid (1995); and Huselid, Becker, and Beatty (2005a, 2005b).

14. Using the list of "The 100 Best Companies to Work for in America" published by *Fortune* in 1998 for their research, Fulmer, Gerhart, and Scott (2003) found that the "100 Best Companies" performed better than a matched sample of firms and also better than the broad market in subsequent years (82 percent cumulative investment returns 1998 to 2000 for the 100 Best vs. 37 percent for the broad market).

15. See Hackman and Oldham (1980); and Morgeson, Delaney-Klinger, and Hemingway (2005).

16. The meta-analysis by Combs, Liu, Hall, and Ketchen (2006) estimates that organizations can increase their performance by 0.20 of a standard unit for each unit increase in HPWP use. Also see Batt and Valcour (2003); Berg, Kalleberg, and Appelbaum (2003); Blasi and Kruse (2006); Eaton (2003); and Gittleman, Horrigan, and Joyce (1998).

17. Drucker (1974, Chapter 34).

18. A current best seller *The Three Signs of a Miserable Job: A Fable for Managers* by Lencioni (2007) is a fable that points to three signs of a miserable job— (1) anonymity, (2) irrelevance, and (3) "immeasurement"—employees not

able to gauge their progress and level of contribution for themselves. The second sign points to the need for people to feel that their job matters to someone, and the first sign can be traced all the way back to the classic "Hawthorne Effect" discovered by Roethlisberger and Dickson (1939). In "The Set-Up-to-Fail Syndrome," Manzoni and Barsoux (1998) state, "What bosses do *not* realize is that their tight controls end up hurting subordinates' performance by undermining their motivation in two ways: first, by depriving subordinates of autonomy on the job and, second, by making them feel undervalued" (p. 106).

19. Zaleznik (2004). Originally published in 1977 and reissued as an HBR Classic in 2004. In contrast, Bennis and Thomas (2002) argue that leaders are made, not born. Based on extensive interviews with 43 executives, they found that every leader, regardless of age, had undergone at least one intense transformational experience, what the authors call a "crucible experience." This is in fact what Zaleznik also found as reported in his article "The Management of Disappointment" (1967).

20. The influence of both nature (biological heritage, genetic makeup) and nurture (life experiences) is well established. George and Jones (2008, p. 42) cite evidence from research on separated identical twins that suggests that about 50 percent of the variation we observe in people's personalities can be attributed to nature, and the other 50 percent reflects the influence of nurture. For the interaction of the person with the situation, see Judge and Kristof-Brown (2004); and Sathe (2003, pp. 96–97).

21. Badaracco and Ellsworth (1989). Bennis and Thomas (2002) found that among the qualities that enable people to remain leaders is a sense of integrity that allows them to distinguish good from evil.

22. George (2003, 2007).

23. Collins (2001a, 2001b).

24. You may aspire to become a Level 5 leader, but we don't yet know how one becomes such a leader as Collins is careful to point out (2001a, p. 37): "My best advice, based on the research, is to begin practicing the other good-to-great disciplines we discovered. . . . There is no guarantee that doing so will turn you into full-fledged Level 5, but it gives you a tangible place to begin."

25. Kotter (1990a, 1990b).

26. Lipman-Blumen (2004).

27. Barnard (1938); Collins and Porras (1996, 1997); Ellsworth (2002); and Selznick (1957). As Sathe and Tyabji (2007, p. 13) conclude: "We have argued that the CEO's new calling is to lead stakeholders to feel a greater sense of responsibility for the enterprise. In striving to do so, CEOs will create higher levels of performance and enthusiasm in and around the enterprise. The central idea—derived from economics, psychology, and philosophy—is

to recognize that employees are the enterprise and must be led to feel its emotional ownership. Treating employees as friends according to Aristotle's third type of friendship is the golden key to their hearts and minds. Transcendent leadership is then possible, and it has the potential to invigorate and ennoble the workplace and lead stakeholders to feel greater responsibility for the enterprise."

28. Drucker (1954).

29. As reported in *The Economist* (May 8, 2004, p. 64), the award-winning documentary, "The Corporation," by three Canadian cocreators depicts capitalism's most important institution as a psychopath: "Like all psychopaths, the firm is singularly self-interested: its purpose is to create wealth for shareholders. And, like all psychopaths, the firm is irresponsible, because it puts others at risk to satisfy its profit-maximization goal, harming employees and customers and damaging the environment."

30. Christensen (1997, p. 133).

31. Lawrence (1954, HBR Classic 1969) is an early account of why people resist change.

32. Jim Collins (personal communication, April 2007).

33. I thank Bill Brockenborough of Chevron Energy Solutions for pointing this out. Attribution on the Web is to Ted Nordhaus and Michael Shellenberger at http://pandemo.livejournal.com/779456.html Thanks also to Claudio Fernández-Aráoz for pointing out that PEA (positive emotional attractors) are much more powerful for change than NEA (negative ones), a finding that he attributes to Richard Boyatzis.

34. Any enterprise—for-profit, nonprofit, government, or volunteer—can use the good-to-great framework in Collins (2001a, 2005) to move forward with positive energy.

35. Collins (2001a, 2005). Also see Hamel and Prahalad (1996).

36. Sathe (2000).

37. The best training takes place on the job. McCall (1998) builds on his prior work that had already demonstrated this and provides a framework for linking the firm's business strategy with the kinds of experiences people need to become future leaders. As Bolt points out, "70 percent of what executives learn is from experience (job experiences), 20 percent from relationships (for example, a boss, coach, mentor), and 10 percent from knowledge (education events, structured learning). Rather than worrying about whether or not these percentages are right, what we need to be thinking about today is how to *accelerate* development in all three of these. That's where the big payoff is" (2005, p. xiv).

38. Drucker (1985) and Sathe (2003).

39. Sathe (2003).

References

Adams, M. G. (2004). *Change your questions change your life: 7 powerful tools for life and work.* San Francisco, CA: Berrett-Koehler.

Adler, N. J., & Gundersen, A. (2008). *International dimensions of organizational behavior* (5th ed.). Dallas, TX: South-Western College Publishing.

Allen, R. W., Madison, D. L., Porter, L. W., Renwick, P. A., & Mayes, B. T. (1979, Fall). Organizational politics: Tactics and characteristics of its actors. *California Management Review, 22*(1), 77–78.

Allport, G. W., Vernon, P. E., & Lindzey, G. (1970). *Manual for the study of values.* Boston, MA: Houghton Mifflin.

Anakwe, U. P., & Greenhaus, J. H. (1999). Effective socialization of employees: Socialization content perspective. *Journal of Managerial Issues, 11*(3), 315–329.

Argyris, C. (1982). *Reasoning, learning, and action.* San Francisco, CA: Jossey-Bass.

Argyris, C., & Schon, D. A. (1974). *Theory in practice.* San Francisco, CA: Jossey-Bass.

Aronson, E. (1976). *The social animal* (2nd ed.). San Francisco, CA: W. H. Freeman.

Aryee, S., Budhwar, P. S., & Chen, Z. X. (2002). Trust as a mediator of the relationship between organizational justice and work outcomes: Test of a social exchange model. *Journal of Organizational Behavior, 23*(3), 267–285.

Asher, D. (2007). *Who gets promoted, who doesn't, and why.* Berkeley, CA: Ten Speed Press.

Ashforth, B., Saks, A., & Lee, R. (1998, July). Socialization and newcomer adjustment: The role of organizational context. *Human Relations, 51*(7), 897–926.

Athos, A. G., & Gabarro, J. J. (1978). *Interpersonal behavior.* Englewood Cliffs, NJ: Prentice-Hall.

Avery, R. W. (1960). Enculturation in industrial research. *IRE Transactions on Engineering Management, 7*, 20–24.

Bachrach, P., & Baratz, M. S. (1962). The two faces of power. *American Political Science Review, 56*(4), 947–952.

Bacharach, S., & Lawler, E. J. (1980). *Power and politics in organizations.* San Francisco, CA: Jossey-Bass.

Badaracco, J. L., Jr. (2002). *Leading quietly: An unorthodox guide to doing the right thing.* Boston, MA: Harvard Business School Press.

Badaracco, J. L., & Ellsworth, R. R. (1989). *Leadership and the quest for integrity.* Boston, MA: Harvard Business School Press.

Ball, M. (2003). @ the entry level: On survival, success, & your calling as a young professional. Los Angeles, CA: Pure Play Press.

Barnard, C. I. (1938). The functions of the executive. Cambridge, MA: Harvard University Press.

Barrick, M. R., Mount, M. K., & Judge, T. A. (2001, March–June). Personality and performance at the beginning of the new millennium: What do we know and where do we go next? International Journal of Selection and Assessment, 9(1–2), 9–30.

Barrick, M. R., & Zimmerman, R. D. (2005, January). Reducing voluntary, avoidable turnover through selection. Journal of Applied Psychology, 90(1), 159–166.

Batt, R., & Valcour, P. M. (2003, April). Human resources practices as predictors of work-family outcomes and employee turnover. Industrial Relations, 42(2), 189–200.

Bellah, R. N., Madsen, R., Sullivan, W. M., Swidler A., & Tipton, S. M. (2008). Habits of the heart: Individualism and commitment in American life. Berkeley: University of California Press.

Bem, D. J. (1970). Beliefs, attitudes, and human affairs. Monterey, CA: Brooks/ Cole Publishing.

Bennis, W. G., & Thomas, R. J. (2002). Geeks and geezers: How era, values and defining moments shape leaders. Boston, MA: Harvard Business School Publishing.

Berg, P., Kalleberg, A. L., & Appelbaum, E. (2003, April). Balancing work and family: The role of high-commitment environments. Industrial Relations, 42(2), 168–188.

Blasi, J. R., & Kruse, D. L. (2006, October). U. S. high-performance work practices at century's end. Industrial Relations, 45(4), 547–578.

Bolles, R. N. (2008). What color is your parachute? Berkeley, CA: Ten Speed Press.

Bolt, J. F. (Ed.). (2005). The future of executive development. Oklahoma City, OK: Executive Development Associates.

Bossidy, R., Charan, R., Burck, C., & Smith, C. (2002). Execution: The discipline of getting things done. New York, NY: Crown Business.

Buckingham, M., & Coffman, C. (1999). First, break all the rules: What the world's greatest managers do differently. New York, NY: Simon & Schuster.

Buckley, M. R., Veres, J. G., Fedor, D. B., Wiese, D. S., & Carraher, S. W. (1998). Investigating newcomer expectations and job-related outcomes. Journal of Applied Psychology, 83(3), 452–461.

Burud, S., & Tumolo, M. (2004). Leveraging the new human capital: Adaptive strategies, results achieved, and stories of transformation. Palo Alto, CA: Davies-Black Publishing.

Butler, T. (2007). Getting unstuck: How dead ends become new paths. Boston, MA: Harvard Business School Press.

Cable D. M., & Edwards J. R. (2004). Complementary and supplementary fit: A theoretical and empirical integration. *Journal of Applied Psychology, 89,* 822–834.

Cable, D. M., & Judge, T. A. (1996, September). Person-organization fit, job choice decisions, and organizational entry. *Organizational Behavior and Human Decision Processes, 67*(3), 294–311.

Cable, D. M., & Parsons, C. K. (2001, Spring). Socialization tactics and person-organization fit. *Personnel Psychology, 54*(1), 1–23.

Cameron, K. E., & Quinn, R. E. (1999). *Diagnosing and changing organizational culture: Based on the competing values framework.* Reading, MA: Addison-Wesley.

Cappelli, P., Constantine, J., & Chadwick, C. (2000, April). It pays to value family: Work and family tradeoffs reconsidered. *Industrial Relations, 39*(2), 175–196.

Carr, A. (2004). *Positive psychology: The science of happiness and human strengths.* Hove, United Kingdom: Brunner-Routledge.

Chao, G. T., & Moon, H. (2005, November). The cultural mosaic: A metatheory for understanding the complexity of culture. *Journal of Applied Psychology, 90*(6), 1128–1140.

Charan, R., Drotter, S., & Noel, J. (2001). *The leadership pipeline: How to build the leadership-powered company.* San Francisco, CA: Jossey-Bass.

Christen, M., Iyer, G., & Soberman, D. (2006, January). Job satisfaction, job performance and effort: A reexamination using agency theory. *Journal of Marketing, 70*(1), 137–150.

Christensen, C. M. (1997). *The innovator's dilemma: When technologies cause great companies to fail.* Boston, MA: Harvard Business School Press.

Cialdini, R. B. (1993). *Influence: Science and practice* (3rd ed.). New York, NY: HarperCollins.

Clawson, J. G., Kotter, J. P., Faux, V. A., & McArthur, C. C. (1992). *Self-assessment and career development* (3rd ed.). Englewood Cliffs, NJ: Prentice Hall.

Collins, J. (2001a). *Good to great.* New York, NY: Harper Business.

Collins, J. (2001b, January). Level 5 leadership: The triumph of humility and fierce resolve. *Harvard Business Review, 79*(1), 66–76.

Collins, J. (2005). *Good to great and the social sectors.* Boulder, CO: Author.

Collins, J., & Porras, J. (1996, September–October). Building your company's vision. *Harvard Business Review, 74*(5), 65–77.

Collins, J., & Porras, J. (1997). *Built to last.* New York, NY: HarperCollins.

Combs, J., Liu, Y., Hall, A., & Ketchen, D. (2006, Autumn). How much do high-performance work practices matter? A meta-analysis of their effects on organizational performance. *Personnel Psychology, 59*(3), 501–528.

Csikszentmihalyi, M. (1990). *Flow: The psychology of optimal experience.* New York, NY: HarperCollins.

Csikszentmihalyi, M. (1996). *Creativity: Flow and the psychology of discovery and invention.* New York, NY: Harper Perennial.

Csikszentmihalyi, M. (2003). *Good business: Leadership, flow and the making of meaning.* New York, NY: Viking.

Damasio, A. (1994). *Descartes' error: Emotion, reason, and the human brain.* New York, NY: G. P. Putnam's Sons.

de Charms, R. (1968). *Personal causation.* New York, NY: Academic Press.

Deutsch, M. (1962). Cooperation and trust: Some theoretical notes. In R. Jones (Ed.), *Nebraska symposium on motivation* (pp. 275–319). Lincoln, OR: University of Nebraska Press.

Dornbush, S. (1955). The military academy as an assimilating institution. *Social Forces, 33*(4), 316–321.

Drago, R., & Hyatt, D. (2003, April). Symposium: The effect of work-family policies on employees and employers. *Industrial Relations, 42*(2), 139–144.

Drucker, P. F. (1954). *The practice of management.* New York, NY: Harper & Row.

Drucker, P. F. (1974). *Management: Tasks, responsibilities, practices.* New York, NY: Harper & Row.

Drucker, P. F. (1985). *Innovation and entrepreneurship.* New York, NY: Harper Business.

Drucker, P. F. (1994, September–October). The theory of the business. *Harvard Business Review, 72*(5), 95–104.

Drucker, P. F. (2005, January). Managing yourself. *Harvard Business Review, 83*(1), 100–109.

Drucker, P. F. (2006). *The effective executive.* New York, NY: HarperCollins.

DuBrin, A. J. (2008). *Human relations for career and personal success* (8th ed.). Upper Saddle River, NJ: Pearson Prentice Hall.

Ducharme, L. J., & Martin, J. K. (2000, May). Unrewarding work, coworker support, and job satisfaction. *Work and Occupations, 27*(2), 223–243.

Eaton, S. C. (2003, April). If you can use them: Flexibility policies, organizational commitment, and perceived performance. *Industrial Relations, 42*(2), 145–167.

Edwards, J. R. (1993, Autumn). Problems with the use of profile similarity indices in the study of congruence in organizational research. *Personnel Psychology, 46*(3), 641–665.

Edwards, J. R. (1996, April). An examination of competing versions of the person-environment fit approach to stress. *Academy of Management Journal, 39*(2), 292–339.

Eisenberger, R., Huntington, R., Hutchison, S., & Sowa, D. (1986). Perceived organizational support. *Journal of Applied Psychology, 71*(3), 500–507.

Ellsworth, R. (2002). *Leading with purpose.* Stanford, CA: Stanford Business Books.

Erdogan, B., & Enders, J. (2007, March). Support from the top: Supervisors' perceived organizational support as a moderator of leader-member exchange to satisfaction and performance relationships. *Journal of Applied Psychology, 92*(2), 321–330.

Fernandez-Araoz, C. (2007). *Great people decisions: Why they matter so much, why they are so hard, and how you can master them.* Hoboken, NJ: John Wiley & Sons.

Ferrin, D. L., & Dirks, K. T. (2003, January). The use of rewards to increase and decrease trust: Mediating processes and differential effects. *Organization Science, 14*(1), 18–31.

Festinger, L. (1957). *A theory of cognitive dissonance.* Evanston, IL: Row, Peterson.

Finkelstein, S. (2003). *Why smart executives fail: And what you can learn from their mistakes.* New York, NY: Portfolio.

Freedman, J. L., & Doob, A. N. (1968). *Deviancy: The psychology of being different.* New York, NY: Academic Press.

Fulmer, I. S., Gerhart, B., & Scott, K. S. (2003). Are the 100 best better? An empirical investigation of the relationship between being a "great place to work" and firm performance. *Personnel Psychology, 56*, 965–993.

Gabarro, J. J. (1978). The development or trust, influence, and expectations. In A. G. Athos & J. J. Gabarro (Eds.), *Interpersonal behavior* (pp. 290–303). Englewood Cliffs, NJ: Prentice-Hall.

Gabarro, J. J. (1979, Winter). Socialization at the top—How CEOs and subordinates evolve interpersonal contacts. *Organizational Dynamics, 7*(3), 2–23.

Gabarro, J. J. (1987). *The dynamics of taking charge.* Boston, MA: Harvard Business School Press.

Gabarro, J. J. (2007, January). When a new manager takes charge. *Harvard Business Review, 85*(1), 104–117.

Gabarro, J. J., & Kotter, J. P. (1980, January–February). Managing your boss. *Harvard Business Review, 58*(1), 92–100.

Gardner, H. (2006). *Multiple intelligences: New horizons.* New York, NY: Basic Books.

George, B. (2003). *Authentic leadership: Rediscovering the secrets to creating lasting value.* San Francisco, CA: Jossey-Bass.

George, B. (2007). *True north: Discover your authentic leadership.* San Francisco, CA: John Wiley & Sons.

George, J. M., & Jones, G. R. (2008). *Understanding and managing organizational behavior* (5th ed.). Upper Saddle River, NJ: Pearson Prentice Hall.

Gittleman, M., Horrigan, M., & Joyce, M. (1998, October). "Flexible" workplace practices: From a nationally representative survey. *Industrial and Labor Relations Review, 52*(1), 99–115.

Gladwell, M. (2005). *Blink: The power of thinking without thinking.* New York, NY: Little, Brown and Company.

Goffman, E. (1961). *Asylums.* Garden City, NY: Doubleday.

Goleman, D. (1995). *Emotional intelligence.* New York, NY: Bantam Books.

Goleman, D. (1998, November–December). What makes a leader? *Harvard Business Review, 76*(6), 93–102.

Greenberg, J, & Baron, R. A. (2008). *Behavior in organizations* (9th ed.). Upper Saddle River, NJ: Pearson Prentice Hall.

Greenhaus, J. H., & Callanan, G. A. (1994). *Career management* (2nd ed.). Fort Worth, TX: Dryden Press.

Guth, W. D., & Tagiuri, R. (1965, September–October). Personal values and corporate strategies. *Harvard Business Review, 43*(5), 123–132.

Hackman, J. R., & Oldham, G. R. (1980). *Work redesign.* Reading, MA: Addison-Wesley.

Hall, D. T., & Chandler, D. E. (2005). Psychological success: When the career is a calling. *Journal of Organizational Behavior, 26,* 155–176.

Hallowell, E. M. (2005, January). Overloaded circuits: Why smart people underperform. *Harvard Business Review, 83*(1), 54–62.

Hamel, G., & Prahalad, C. K. (1996). *Competing for the future.* Boston, MA: Harvard Business School Press.

Handy, C. (1978). *Gods of management.* London, United Kingdom: Souvenir Press.

Harrison, R. (1972, May–June). Understanding your organization's character. *Harvard Business Review, 50*(3), 119–128.

Harvard Business Review. (2002). *Harvard business review on managing your career.* Boston, MA: Harvard Business School Press.

Harvard Business Review. (2005). *Harvard business review on managing yourself.* Boston, MA: Harvard Business School Press.

Harvard Business School. (2004). *Coaching and mentoring: How to develop top talent and achieve stronger performance.* Boston, MA: Author.

Herrick, J. A. (2004). *Argumentation: Understanding and shaping arguments.* State College, PA: Strata Publishing.

Herzberg, F., Mausner, B., & Snyderman, B. B. (1959). *The motivation to work.* New York, NY: Wiley.

Heslin, P. A. (2005, February). Conceptualizing and evaluating career success. *Journal of Organizational Behavior, 26*(2), 113–136.

Hill, L. A. (2003). *Becoming a manager: How new managers master the challenges of leadership* (2nd ed.). Boston, MA: Harvard Business School Press.

Hill, L. A. (2007, January). Becoming the boss. *Harvard Business Review, 85*(1), 48–56.

Hofstede, G. (1980a). *Culture's consequences: International differences in work-related values.* Beverly Hills, CA: Sage.

Hofstede, G. (1980b, Summer). Motivation, leadership and organization: Do American theories apply abroad? *Organizational Dynamics, 9*(1), 42–63.

Hollander, E. P. (1958, March). Conformity, status, and idiosyncrasy credit. *Psychological Review, 65*(2), 117–127.

Holton, E. F., III, & Naquin, S. S. (2001). *How to succeed in your first job: Tips for new college graduates.* San Francisco, CA: Berrett-Koehler.

Hughes, C. L., & Flowers, V. S. (1978). *Value system analysis theory and management application.* Dallas, TX: Center for Value Research.

Hughes, E. C. (1958). *Men and their work.* New York, NY: Free Press.

Hurtz, G. M., & Donovan, J. J. (2000). Personality and job performance: The big five revisited. *Journal of Applied Psychology, 85*(6), 869–879.

Huselid, M. A. (1995, June). The impact of human resource management practices on turnover, productivity, and corporate financial performance. *Academy of Management Journal, 38*(3), 635–672.

Huselid, M. A., Becker, B. E., & Beatty, R. W. (2005a). A players or A positions? *Harvard Business Review, 83*(12), 110–117.

Huselid, M. A., Becker, B. E., & Beatty, R. W. (2005b). *The workforce scorecard: Managing human capital to execute strategy.* Boston, MA: Harvard Business School Press.

Ibarra, H. (2004). *Working identity: Unconventional strategies for reinventing your career.* Boston, MA: Harvard Business School Press.

Ibarra, H., & Hunter, M. (2007, January). How leaders create and use networks. *Harvard Business Review, 85*(1), 40–47.

Janis, I. L. (1972). *Victims of groupthink.* Boston, MA: Houghton Mifflin.

Janis, I. L., & Wheeler, D. (1978, May). Thinking clearly about career choice. *Psychology Today, 11*(12), 66.

Judge, T. A., Heller, D., & Mount, M. K. (2002). Five-factor model of personality and job satisfaction: A meta-analysis. *Journal of Applied Psychology, 87*(3), 530–541.

Judge, T. A., & Kristof-Brown, A. (2004). Personality, interactional psychology, and person-organization fit. In B. Schneider & D. B. Smith (Eds.), *Personality and organizations* (pp. 87–109). Mahwah, NJ: Lawrence Erlbaum.

Judge, T. A., Thoresen, C. J., Bono, J. E., & Patton, G. K. (2001). The job satisfaction-job performance relationship: A qualitative and quantitative review. *Psychological Bulletin, 127*(3), 376–407.

Kanter, R. M. (1977). *Men and women of the corporation.* New York, NY: Basic Books.

Kaye, B., & Jordan-Evans, S. (2003). *Love it, don't leave it: 26 ways to get what you want at work.* San Francisco, CA: Berrett-Koehler.

Kelman, H. C. (1958, March). Compliance, identification, and internalization: Three processes of attitude change. *Conflict Resolution, 2*(1), 51–60.

Kiesler, C. A., & Kiesler, S. B. (1969). *Conformity.* Reading, MA: Addison-Wesley.

Kim, T. Y., Cable, D. M., & Kim, S. P. (2005, March). Socialization tactics, employee proactivity, and person-organization fit. *Journal of Applied Psychology, 90*(2), 232–241.

Kluckhohn, C. (1951). Values and value orientations in the theory of action. In T. Parsons & E. A. Shils (Eds.), *Toward a general theory of action* (pp. 388–433). Cambridge, MA: Harvard University Press.

Kolbe, K. (1990–1997). *The conative connection: Uncovering the link between who you are and how you perform.* Reading, MA: Addison-Wesley.

Korman, A. (1968, December). Task success, task popularity and self-esteem as influences on task liking. *Journal of Applied Psychology, 52*(6, Pt. 1), 484–490.

Kotter, J. P. (1977, July–August). Power, dependence, and effective management. *Harvard Business Review, 55*(4), 125–36.

Kotter, J. P. (1982). *The general managers.* New York, NY: Free Press.

Kotter, J. P. (1990a). *Force for change: How leadership differs from management.* New York, NY: Free Press.

Kotter, J. P. (1990b, May–June). What leaders really do. *Harvard Business Review, 68*(3), 103–111.

Kotter, J. P., & Lawrence, P. (1974). *Mayors in action.* New York, NY: John Wiley & Sons.

Kristof-Brown, A. L., Zimmerman, R. D., & Johnson, E. C. (2005). Consequences of individuals' fit at work: A meta-analysis of person-job, person-organization, person-group, and person-supervisor fit. *Personnel Psychology, 58*(2), 281–342.

Lawler, E. E., III, & Rhode, J. G. (1976). *Information and control in organizations.* Santa Monica, CA: Goodyear Publishing.

Lawrence, P. R. (1954, May–June). How to deal with resistance to change [reprinted as HBR Classic, 1969, January–February]. *Harvard Business Review,* 77–86.

Lawrence, P. R., & Lorsch, J. W. (1967). *Organization and environment: Managing differentiation and integration.* Boston, MA: Division of Research, Harvard Business School.

Lee, J. A. (1966, March–April). Cultural analysis of overseas operations. *Harvard Business Review, 44*(2), 106–114.

Leeds, R. (1964). The absorption of protest: A working paper. In W. W. Cooper, H. J. Leavitt, & M. W. Shelly, II (Eds.), *New perspectives in organizational research* (pp. 115–133). New York, NY: John Wiley & Sons.

Lencioni, P. (2007). *The three signs of a miserable job: A fable for managers.* San Francisco, CA: Jossey-Bass.

Levinson, H. (1972). *Organizational diagnosis.* Cambridge, MA: Harvard University Press.

Lewicki, R. J. (1981, Autumn). Organizational seduction: Building commitment to organizations. *Organizational Dynamics, 10*(2), 5–21.

Lewicki, R. J., McAllister, D. J., & Bies, R. J. (1998). Trust and distrust: New relationships and realities [Special topic forum on trust in and between organizations]. *Academy of Management Review, 23*(3), 438–458.

Lipman-Blumen, J. (2004). *The allure of toxic leaders: Why we follow destructive bosses and corrupt politicians—and how we can survive them*. Oxford, United Kingdom: Oxford University Press.

Livingstone, L. P., Nelson, D. L., & Barr, S. H. (1997). Person-environment fit and creativity: An examination of supply-value and demand-ability versions of fit. *Journal of Management, 23*(2), 119–146.

Locke, E. (2004). Goal-setting theory and its applications to the world of business. *Academy of Management Executive, 18*(4), 124–125.

Louis, M. (1980, June). Surprise and sense making: What newcomers experience in entering unfamiliar organizational settings. *Administrative Science Quarterly, 25*(2), 226–251.

Lounsbury, J. W., Moffitt, L., Gibson, L. W., Drost, A. W., & Stevens, M. (2007, June). An investigation of personality traits in relation to job and career satisfaction of information technology professionals. *Journal of Information Technology, 22*(2), 174–183.

Lubit, R. (2002). The long-term organizational impact of destructively narcissistic managers. *Academy of Management Executive, 16*(1), 127–138.

Lyman, L. M., & Scott, M. B. (1970). *A sociology of the absurd*. New York, NY: Meredith.

Manzoni, J.-F., & Barsoux, J.-L. (1998). The set-up-to-fail syndrome. *Harvard Business Review, 76*(3), 101–113.

Martin, J., & Siehl, C. (1983, Autumn). Organizational culture and counterculture: An uneasy symbiosis. *Organizational Dynamics, 12*(2), 52–64.

Martin, R. (1993, November–December). Changing the mind of the corporation. *Harvard Business Review, 71*(6), 81–94.

Martin, R. (2007). *The opposable mind: How successful leaders win through integrative thinking*. Boston, MA: Harvard Business School Press.

Maslow, A. H. (1943). A theory of human motivation. *Psychological Review, 50*, 370–396.

Maslow, A. H. (1971). *The farther reaches of human nature*. New York, NY: Viking Penguin Books.

Maslow, A. H., Stephens, D. C., & Heil, G. (1998). *Maslow on management*. New York, NY: Wiley.

McCall, M. W., Jr. (1998). *High flyers: Developing the next generation of leaders*. Boston, MA: Harvard Business School Press.

McClelland, D. (1961). *The achieving society*. Princeton, NJ: Van Nostrand Reinhold.

McGuire, W. J. (1964). Inducing resistance to persuasion: Some contemporary approaches. In L. Berkowitz (Ed.), *Advances in experimental social psychology* (Vol. 1, pp. 191–229). New York, NY: Academic Press.

McMurry, R. N. (1963, May–June). Conflicts in human values. *Harvard Business Review, 41*(3), 130–145.

Menkes, J. (2005). *Executive intelligence: What all great leaders have.* New York, NY: HarperCollins.

Milgram, S. (1963). Behavioral study of obedience. *Journal of Abnormal and Social Psychology, 67*(4), 371–378.

Milgram, S. (1965). Some conditions of obedience and disobedience to authority. *Human Relations, 18*(1), 57–76.

Mitchell, T. R., Holtom, B. C., Lee, T. W., Sablynski, C. J., & Erez, M. (2001, December). Why people stay: Using job embeddedness to predict voluntary turnover. *Academy of Management Journal, 44*(6), 1102–1121.

Montgomery, C. E. (1996, January). Organizational fit is key to job success. *HR Magazine, 41*(1), 94–96.

Moore, W. (1962). *The conduct of the corporation.* New York, NY: Random House.

Morgeson, F. P., Delaney-Klinger, K., & Hemingway, M. A. (2005, March). The importance of job autonomy, cognitive ability, and job-related skill for predicting role breadth and job performance. *Journal of Applied Psychology, 90*(2), 399–406.

Motowidlo, S. J., & Van Scotter, J. R. (1994, August). Evidence that task performance should be distinguished from contextual performance. *Journal of Applied Psychology, 79*(4), 475–480.

Myers, D. G. (1992). *The pursuit of happiness: Discovering the pathway to fulfillment, well-being, and enduring personal joy.* New York, NY: Quill.

Nelson, B. (2001). *Please don't just do what I tell you! Do what needs to be done.* New York, NY: Hyperion.

O'Day, R. (1974, July). Intimidation rituals: Reactions to reform. *Journal of Applied Behavioral Science, 10*(3), 373–386.

Odiorne, G. (1974). *Management and the activity trap: How to avoid it and how to get out of it.* New York, NY: Harper & Row.

O'Reilly, C. A., III, & Caldwell, D. F. (1981). The commitment and job tenure of new employees: Some evidence of postdecisional justification. *Administrative Science Quarterly, 23*(4), 597–616.

O'Reilly, C. A., III, Chatman, J., & Caldwell, D. F. (1991). People and organizational culture: A profile comparison approach to assessing person-organization fit. *Academy of Management Journal, 34*(3), 487–516.

Organ, D. W., & Lingl, A. (1995). Personality, satisfaction, and organizational citizenship behavior. *Journal of Social Psychology, 135*(3), 339–350.

Ott, B., Blacksmith, N., & Royal, K. (2007, December 13). Job seekers ask: Who's the boss? *Gallup Management Journal Online.* Retrieved from http://gmj.gallup.com/content/103114/Job-Seekers-Ask-Whos-Boss.aspx

Parasuraman, A., Berry, L. L., & Zeithaml, V. A. (1991). Refinement and reassessment of the SERVQUAL scale. *Journal of Retailing, 67*(4), 420–450.

Pfeffer, J. (1981). *Power in organizations.* Marshfield, MA: Pitman.

Pfeffer, J., & Sutton, R. I. (2006). *Hard facts, dangerous half-truths, & total non-sense: Profiting from evidence-based management.* Boston, MA: Harvard Business School Press.

Pondy, L., Frost, P. J., Morgan, G., & Dandridge, T. C. (Eds.) (1983). *Organizational symbolism.* Greenwich, CT: JAI Press.

Rath, T. (2007). *Strengthsfinder 2.0.* New York, NY: Gallup Press.

Reardon, K. K. (2007, January). Courage as a skill. *Harvard Business Review, 85*(1), 48–56.

Rhoads, L., & Eisenberger, R. (2002, August). Perceived organizational support: A review of the literature. *Journal of Applied Psychology, 87*(4), 698–714.

Rhoads, L., Eisenberger, R., & Armeli, S. (2001). Affective commitment to the organization: The contribution of perceived organizational support. *Journal of Applied Psychology, 86*(5), 825–836.

Roethlisberger, F. J., & Dickson, W. J. (1939). *Management and the worker.* Cambridge, MA: Harvard University Press.

Rokeach, M. (1968). *Beliefs, attitudes, and values.* San Francisco, CA: Jossey-Bass.

Rollag, K., Parise, S., & Cross, R. (2005, Winter). Getting new hires up to speed quickly. *MIT Sloan Management Review, 46*(2), 35–41.

Rotter, J. B. (1966). Generalized expectancies for internal versus external control of reinforcement. *Psychological Monographs: General and Applied, 80*(1, Whole No. 609), 1–28.

Salancik, G. R. (1977, Summer). Commitment is too easy. *Organizational Dynamics, 6*(1), 62–80.

Sathe, V. (1982). *Controller involvement in management.* Englewood Cliffs, NJ: Prentice-Hall.

Sathe, V. (1985). *Culture and related corporate realities: Text, cases, and readings on organizational entry, establishment, and change.* Homewood, IL: Richard D. Irwin.

Sathe, V. (2000, May–June). Creating change in mindset and behavior. *Ivey Business Journal,* 83–89.

Sathe, V. (2003). *Corporate entrepreneurship: Top managers and new business creation.* Cambridge, United Kingdom: Cambridge University Press.

Sathe, V., & Tyabji, H. (2007, Fall). A new dimension of leadership. *Leader to Leader, 46,* 11–14.

Schein, E. H. (1964). Personal change through interpersonal relationships. In W. G. Bennis, E. H. Schein, D. E. Berlew, & F. L. Steele (Eds.), *Interpersonal dynamics: Essays and readings on human interaction* (pp. 357–394). Homewood, IL: Dorsey Press.

Schein, E. H. (1968, Winter). Organizational socialization and the profession of management. *Industrial Management Review, 9*(2), 1–16.

Schein, E. H. (1978). *Career dynamics.* Reading, MA: Addison-Wesley.

Schein, E. H. (1983, Summer). The role of the founder in creating organizational culture. *Organizational Dynamics, 12*(1), 13–28.

Schein, E. H. (1985). *Organizational culture and leadership: A dynamic view.* San Francisco, CA: Jossey-Bass.

Schein, E. H. (1995). *Career survival: Strategic job and role planning.* Johannesburg, South Africa: Pfeiffer & Company.

Schein, E. H. (1996). Career anchors revisited. Implications for career development in the 21st century. *Academy of Management Executive, 10*(4), 80–88.

Schein, E. H. (2006). *Career anchors: Self-assessment* (3rd ed.). San Francisco, CA: Pfeiffer.

Schneider, B. (1987, Autumn). The people make the place. *Personnel Psychology, 40*(3), 437–453.

Schneider, B. (2001, January). Fits about fit. *Applied Psychology: An International Review, 50*(1), 141–152.

Schneider, B., Goldstein, H. W., & Smith, D. B. (1995). The ASA framework: An update. *Personnel Psychology, 48*(4), 747–773.

Seligman, M. E. P. (2002). *Authentic happiness: Using the new positive psychology to realize your potential for lasting fulfillment.* New York, NY: Free Press.

Selznick, P. (1957). *Leadership in administration.* New York, NY: Harper & Row.

Shaw, J. B., & Gupta, N. (2004). Job complexity, performance, and well-being: When does supplies-values fit matter? *Personnel Psychology, 57*, 847–879.

Sherif, M. (1936). *The social psychology of social norms.* New York, NY: Harper & Row.

Siehl, C., & Martin, J. (1981, September). *Learning organizational culture* [Working paper]. Stanford, CA: Stanford Graduate School of Business.

Simon, H. A. (1973, May–June). Applying information technology to organization design. *Public Administration Review, 33*(3), 268–278.

Smart, B., & Smart, G. (2005) *Topgrading: How to hire, coach and keep A players.* Dallas, TX: Pritchett.

Soelberg, P. O. (1967). Unprogrammed decision making. *Industrial Management Review, 8*(2), 19–29.

Spranger, E. (1928). *Types of men* (P. Pigors, Trans.). Halle, Germany: Niemeyer.

Springbelt, B. M. (1958). Factors affecting the final decision in the employment interview. *Canadian Journal of Psychology, 12*, 13–22.

Staw, B. M. (2004). The dispositional approach to job attitudes: An empirical and conceptual review. In B. Schneider & D. B. Smith (Eds.), *Personality and organizations* (pp. 163–191). Mahwah, NJ: Lawrence Erlbaum.

Staw, B. M., & Cohen-Charash, Y. (2005). The dispositional approach to job satisfaction: More than a mirage, but not yet an oasis. *Journal of Organizational Behavior, 26*, 59–78.

Staw, B. M., & Ross, J. (1985). Stability in the midst of change: A dispositional approach to job attitudes. *Journal of Applied Psychology, 70*(3), 469–480.

Stewart, R. (1979, Autumn). Managerial agendas: Reactive or proactive? *Organizational Dynamics, 8*(2), 34–47.

Stewart, R. (1982). *Choices for the manager.* Englewood Cliffs, NJ: Prentice-Hall.

Stone, F. M. (2007). *Coaching, counseling, & mentoring: How to choose & use the right techniques to boost employee performance.* New York, NY: AMACOM.

Sutton, R. (2007). *The no asshole rule: Building a civilized workplace and surviving one that isn't.* New York, NY: Warner Business Books.

Thompson, J. A. (2005, September). Proactive personality and job performance: A social capital perspective. *Journal of Applied Psychology, 90*(5), 1011–1017.

Ulrich, D., Kerr, S., & Ashkenas, R. (2002). *The GE work-out: How to implement GE's revolutionary method for busting bureaucracy & attacking organizational problems—fast!* New York, NY: McGraw-Hill.

Usheroff, R. (2004). *Customize your career: How to develop a winning strategy to move up, move ahead or move on.* New York, NY: McGraw-Hill.

Van Dyne, L., & Pierce, J. L. (2004, June). Psychological ownership and feelings of possession: Three field studies predicting employee attitudes and organizational citizenship behavior. *Journal of Organizational Behavior, 25*(4), 439–459.

van Gennep, A. (1960). *The rites of passage.* Chicago, IL: University of Chicago Press.

Van Maanen, J. (1976). Breaking in: Socialization to work. In R. Dubin (Ed.), *Handbook of work, organization, and society* (pp. 67–130). Skokie, IL: Rand McNally.

Van Maanen, J. (1978, Summer). People processing: Strategies of organizational socialization. *Organizational Dynamics, 7*(1), 18–36.

Van Maanen, J. (1984). *Business school cultures and corporate America: Careers and the MBA* (13th ed.). Holbrook, MA: Bob Adams.

Van Vianen, A. E. M. (2000, Spring). Person-organization fit: The match between newcomers' and recruiters' preferences for organizational cultures. *Personnel Psychology, 53*(1), 113–149.

Verquer, M. L., Beehr, T. A., & Wagner, S. H. (2003). A meta-analysis of relations between person-organization fit and work attitudes. *Journal of Vocational Behavior, 63,* 473–489.

Wademan, D. (2004). *Remember who you are: Life stories that inspire the heart and mind.* Boston, MA: Harvard Business School Press.

Wall, B. (2000, November). Working relationships: The simple truth about getting along with friends and foes at work. *HR Magazine, 45*(11), 182–184.

Walton, R. E. (1968). *Social and psychological aspects of verification, inspection, and international assurance.* West Lafayette, IN: Purdue University Press.

Walton, R. E. (1969). *Interpersonal peacemaking: Confrontation and third party consultation.* Reading, MA: Addison-Wesley.

Wanberg, C. R., & Kammeyer-Mueller, J. D. (2000). Predictors and outcomes of in the socialization process. *Journal of Applied Psychology, 85*(3), 373–385.

Wanous, J. P. (1980). *Organizational entry.* Reading, MA: Addison-Wesley.

Wanous, J. P. (1989). Realistic job preview: Ten tough choices. *Personnel Psychology, 42*(1), 117–134.

Wanous, J. P., Poland, T. D., Premack, S. L., & Davis, K. S. (1992). The effects of met expectations on newcomer attitudes and behaviors: A review and meta-analysis. *Journal of Applied Psychology, 77*(3), 288–297.

Watkins, M. (2003). *The first 90 days: Critical success strategies for new leaders at all levels.* Boston, MA: Harvard Business School Press.

Weitz, J. (1956, August). Job expectancy and survival. *Journal of Applied Psychology, 40*(4), 245–247.

Wilson, T. (2002). *Strangers to ourselves: Discovering the adaptive unconscious.* Cambridge, MA: Belknap Press of Harvard University Press.

Wrzesniewski, A. (2003). Finding positive meaning in work. In K. S. Cameron, J. E. Dutton, & R. E. Quinn (Eds.), *Positive organizational scholarship* (pp. 296–308). San Francisco, CA: Berrett-Koehler.

Wrzesniewski, A., & Dutton, J. E. (2001). Crafting a job: Revisioning employees as active crafters of their work. *Academy of Management Review, 26*(2), 179–201.

Wrzesniewski, A., McCauley, C., Rozin, P., & Schwartz, B. (1997, March). Jobs, careers, and callings: People's relations to their work. *Journal of Research in Personality, 31*(1), 21–33.

Yoneshige, K. S. (2005). *Flow and friendship in the workplace and its effects on job satisfaction* (Unpublished master's thesis). Claremont Graduate University, Claremont, CA.

Zaleznik, A. (1967, November–December). Management of disappointment. *Harvard Business Review, 45*(6), 59–70.

Zaleznik, A. (2004, January). Managers and leaders: Are they different? *Harvard Business Review, 82*(1), 74–81.

Zimbardo, P. G. (1971). The pathology of imprisonment. *Society, 9,* 4–8.

Index

The letter *f* following a page number denotes a figure.

Announcing the Business Expert Press Digital Library

Concise e-books business students need for classroom and research

This book can also be purchased in an e-book collection by your library as

- a one-time purchase,
- that is owned forever,
- allows for simultaneous readers,
- has no restrictions on printing, and
- can be downloaded as PDFs from within the library community.

Our digital library collections are a great solution to beat the rising cost of textbooks. E-books can be loaded into their course management systems or onto student's e-book readers. The **Business Expert Press** digital libraries are very affordable, with no obligation to buy in future years. For more information, please visit **www.businessexpertpress.com/librarians**. To set up a trial in the United States, please contact **sales@businessexpertpress.com**.

Printed in the USA
CPSIA information can be obtained
at www.ICGtesting.com
BVHW051441210823
668746BV00003B/10